I0190196

Answers to The Top Homeschooling Questions

Helping Parents Homeschool with Confidence

Julia Groves   Donna Goff

ISBN: 978-1-7354632-1-6

Cover design by: Rory R. Groves

Printed in the United States of America

MAGNITUDESTUDIOS

DEDICATION

This book is dedicated to all the amazing parents out there
who have question about homeschooling. You are not alone.

Answers to The Top Homeschooling Questions

CONTENTS

Title Page
Copyright
Dedication

	Introduction	I
1	Is Homeschooling Legal?	Pg 1
2	What is the Best Homeschool Curriculum?	Pg 15
3	Will Homeschooling Affect My Child's Social Development?	Pg 43
4	How Long Do You Need to Spend Homeschooling Each Day?	Pg 51
5	How Do I Actually Homeschool My Children?	Pg 59
6	What Do You Do if Your Child Doesn't Want to Be Homeschooled?	Pg 79
7	Will Homeschooling Put My Children Behind?	Pg 111
8	How do I Prepare My High Schooler for College?	Pg 105
9	How Do I Prepare My High Schooler for a Career?	Pg 115
10	How do I homeschool Without Having it Take Over My Life?	Pg 125
	In Closing	Pg 145
	About the Authors	Pg 146

INTRODUCTION

This is book two in our Homeschooling Basics Series. In the last book, *A Beginner's Guide for Homeschooling*, we talked about how to set up a successful homeschool by making sure you have a solid foundation.

In this book, we will be providing answers to the top homeschooling questions and concerns that are commonly asked by parents looking into homeschooling. In doing so, it is our hope that you will be able to move forward in your homeschool journey with confidence.

Yes, choosing to homeschool your children is a big decision and commitment. Which is why having questions is natural. It is important to know that you are not alone. In fact, you aren't the first or the last to ask these same questions before starting on your homeschool adventure.

Before we jump in and start answering these important homeschool questions, we would like to take a moment to introduce ourselves and our homeschooling background.

Hi, I am Donna Goff and I began homeschooling in the 1980s. Before I had children, I had never planned to homeschool. So, when I came to homeschooling, I did so reluctantly. It was before the internet and so I only had bookstores and libraries as my sources to figure it out. There were no support groups within about eighty miles! Because homeschooling was not my plan, I had no real plan except to pick up where they left off. I learned the hard way that this is not how to go about beginning homeschooling. This lack of planning resulted in my older children being in and out of public school.

My story would be really short had I firmly settled earlier on whether to either homeschool or public school. If I had it to do over, I would homeschool all of my children from the beginning, through high school, and not just my younger four children. I share my story, because I feel it pertains a lot to this book, to know my journey. I write this in hopes that you will benefit from my experiences.

When I only had two sons and a daughter, I found myself drawn into the early learning philosophy. I took a live week long detailed course in early childhood development. It was focused on how to enhance my children's development and early learning. The things I learned during that time have benefited all of my children. However, a lot of the early learning I found to be too tedious or not natural, as they involved flash cards. I did take the principles of clear focused repetition into my life and in teaching my children. When my daughter was two, we tried doing a play based preschool. All the moms wanted to add academics. As we did not know any better, we added academics. We did preschool for one semester.

Later, I had four more children but armed with more information, I chose not to do preschool at home, nor did I send my children to preschool. I focused more on providing support for healthy development.

My older three children attended kindergarten. I had no idea the law did not require it in the state where I lived. In talking to the principal, he suggested I homeschool! I gave him my notice and two weeks later I started homeschooling my oldest, he was in fourth grade.

We moved and by Christmas I was homeschooling all of them, kinder, third, and fourth grade. That summer I had my fourth child and because of this sent my oldest children back to public school where they attended for the next two years. I had my fifth child and decided to try homeschooling my children again. However, before long, I was exhausted and sleep deprived from a newborn. My husband re-enrolled our older children in public school. I must say I felt guilty and felt like I had failed.

We moved to Utah. I enrolled my three oldest children in public school. However a few months later my daughter begged to just be homeschooled. I understood why she requested to be homeschooled so I agreed to her request. As we left the school that day, we walked by the kindergarten classroom. I pointed it out to her younger sister who replied, "That's fine for them mom, I have something better."

At that instant, I realized I was into homeschooling for the long haul. I invested time in learning about models, philosophies, methods, and connecting with other homeschoolers. I had my sixth child.

My oldest two who didn't want to be homeschooled, chose to do independent study and graduated from high school early. I then had a seventh child. My oldest daughter was homeschooled from sixth grade through graduation. My youngest four children were homeschooled to adulthood.

In this book, I want to share from my experience and help you to begin your homeschool journey. Starting out right can mean a world of difference in how your homeschool flows.

Hi, my name is Julia Groves (I am Donna Goff's oldest daughter). As my mother previously stated, my first personal experience with homeschooling was when I was in kindergarten when my parents for a brief time pulled my older brothers out of the public school system (due to issues at their school) and opted to homeschool them. I enjoyed joining in on their studies. I have a particular memory from that time of my father teaching my older brothers and I how to add large numbers together. He taught us on this huge white board. I remember feeling so grown up that I knew how to add really big numbers together.

Anyway, while that was my first homeschool experience, my official homeschool journey didn't begin for several more years. It began in the middle of my 6th grade year. That is when I begged my mother one day to let me come home to be homeschooled full time. There were a number of reasons for this personal request. The main one being I had no desire to skip another grade (which was being discussed) as I was getting bullied enough for having already done so at my last school.

I decided that I wanted to come home and take charge of my own education. I wanted to really study the subjects I was interested in, rather than just skimming the surface as we were doing in school. I wanted peace away from all the bullies. My mother seeing the writing on the wall agreed to my request and that's how I ended up being homeschooled from the 6th-grade year through high school. (Though I did take a few classes at our local high school with my friends. I even performed in a school play at our local high school thanks to the kindness a understanding drama teacher)

Looking back I have never regretted my decision to be homeschooled even though it came with it's own set of trials. (The main one being that homeschooling wasn't as widespread or accepted back then, so I got a lot of push back from my friends and their parents.)

No, I never doubted or regretted my choice to be homeschooled. In fact, I am very grateful I had the opportunity.

Later on, after attending a couple semesters at private liberal arts college I taught for a short time at private elementary school before stepping away from formally teaching in order to raise my own family. However, through the years I have enjoyed speaking at various Homeschool conferences to both youth and adults.

Now I have 3 kids of my own who I am currently homeschooling together with my husband. I have to say that homeschooling isn't always the easiest educational choice, but it can be the most rewarding. I love teaching my kids and learning from them. But what I really love is that the world is our school. We can go anywhere and learn as we go. We have freedom.

Yay, so now, let's get to answering those important homeschool questions we know you have..

1. IS HOMESCHOOLING LEGAL?

While in some countries in the world, homeschooling your children is not a legal option, thankfully, here in the United States, it is legal.

Though the legal requirements and regulations do vary from state to state, it is totally legal in all fifty states to homeschool.

You just need to make sure that you are in full compliance with your states homeschool laws.

HOW DO I FIND OUT THE LEGAL REQUIREMENTS TO HOMESCHOOL WHERE I LIVE?

In our first book, *A Beginner's Guide for Homeschooling*, we discussed at length issues to pay attention to when looking at homeschool laws.

We recommend going to the Homeschool Legal Defence Association (https://hslda.org/) to find out what the current laws and regulations are for homeschooling in your state. They are great at keeping up on the homeschool laws and legal issues across the United States.

You can also contact your specific state's homeschool association website to get a link to your current state laws for homeschooling.

AM I REQUIRED TO KEEP A DETAILED HOMESCHOOL RECORD FOR EACH CHILD?

This is a good question. Some states do require detailed homeschool records to be kept. Some states do not require you to keep a detailed homeschool record. If your state requires detailed homeschooled records to be kept, please comply. You do not EVER want to be found not complying with state homeschool laws.

We highly encourage you to keep detailed homeschool records, even if your state does not require them. Besides being able to show those records if the need ever arises, these records can be very useful to you and your children.

Records can be a great resource for kids to go back and refresh upon subject material they have previously covered. They can also help build your children's confidence as they see all they have accomplished.

Your records for younger children, below high school age, can be simple. A single page in a notebook can have two sections on the front side of the paper. Place a date on the top of the page.

FAMILY or TOGETHER.

Below that heading, list every learning experience you did together.

TUTORING & MENTORING

Child's name

Under their name, list everything you taught them one on one that day.

On the back of the paper have it divided by each CHILD'S

NAME.
Have the child keep track of learning activities and return to report to you before dinner. Then jot down on the back of the paper, their independent learning.

SAMPLE OF PREK & HOMESCHOOLED GRADE SCHOOL CHILDREN:

---

15 September 2020

TOGETHER:

Read aloud and Discussion - Luke 10:38 - 42

Literature Read Aloud - Little Men Chapter 5.

Science - Nature Walk and Nature Study

History - Story of Liberty Chapter 5

Art History: Carl Heinrich Bloch & Art Appreciation: Christ and the Children

TUTORING & MENTORING

Andy (4)
Read Aloud - Benjamin West and His Cat Grimalkin Chapter 4 (pg 26 to 30).

Math - Matching- A Game of Dominios

Peter (6)
Reading Lesson - 100 Easy Lessons - Lesson 4

Math Lesson - Math for Your 1st and 2nd Grader lesson 4

Writing - Learning to form the upper and lower case D.

Izzy (10)
Reading Lesson - Izzy read aloud "Apple Pip Princess" by Jane Ray
Math Lesson - Math for Your 1st and 2nd Grader lesson 40 Counting & Writing Numbers 1-200

Writing - copy work - "Where you tend a rose, a thistle cannot grow."

Anne (11)
Reading Lesson - Anne narrating the story of the Princess Academy by Shannon Hale (she completed yesterday) and discussed the story.

Math Lesson - Anne demonstrating long division on the white board.

Writing - Copy Work - A passage from Princess Academy, Record in her notebook her reading of Princess Academy.

------------------------------ flip to back side --------------------------

INTEREST LED

Andrew - Building with legos

Peter- Drawing Dinosaurs for his Dinosaur book and family presentation

Lizzy- Began reading *Pollyanna*
      Worked ahead and did Math Lesson 41 Writing Words for Numbers 1-50
      Practiced her Piano - Twinkle Twinkle Little Star

Anne- Wrote a book report on *Princess Academy* to place in her portfolio.
      Worked on writing a story - *My Friend in the Mirror*
      Practiced long division on the white board.
      Practiced her Piano - *Happy Farmer* by Suzuki

Once children can read and write, they can begin keeping their own learning record in a portfolio or binder. Have them meet with you and add to your record what they did for interest led learning.

Once youth are middle-school age, you will want to have them keep their own learning log, meet with you and discuss each entry about what they are learning.

DO MY CHILDREN HAVE TO DO YEARLY STATE TESTING?

Here again, some states require yearly testing, while others only require official testing every-other-year.

As of this writing, about twenty-five states require some sort of testing or portfolio evaluation. The other twenty-five states do not require any official testing at all, unless you choose to place your children back into the public or private school system. At which point, they may test for placement purposes. However, children are usually placed with other children their age.

Some school districts pay for the testing, but in many states, the family covers the costs. Several states allow for an alternate testing by a private entity outside the school system. Other states offer alternate evaluation by portfolio. Please check your state law to find out what is required where you live.

Some parents want to have their child tested, to make sure their child is on par with peers. Yet it is important to note that most peers may not be a grade level.

We need to understand there is a vast difference between teaching and learning. All children are taught the same thing at the same age, but not all children actually master the information.

Most states pass children to the next grade, even though they may be two years below grade level. Many states set the bar below grade level for testing for homeschoolers. It would not be fair to require homeschoolers to make a hurdle that their public school peers do not have to clear.

Even though some parents unschool and others take a one room school approach, in states where testing is required, homeschoolers usually average above the 80th percentile. This is even though many homeschoolers are not using common core grade based curriculum.

IF YOUR STATE DOES NOT REQUIRE ANNUAL TESTING, SHOULD YOU TEST?

Schools spend a lot of time teaching to the test. It is because of this, that most children do not gain proficiency before moving forward. Children who are between two years below grade level to two years above grade level, tend to be moved forward. Most children are moved to the next grade, by age, and not by knowledge acquisition or skill attainment.

It is easy for parents to assume that all children moving ahead have learned everything taught in their previous grade. In reality, this is not the case.

Finland has one of the best school systems in the world. Their students are not constantly given standardized tests throughout their school years.

They do one standardized test at the end of their compulsory school, at age sixteen. Yet, their students consistently outperform ours year after year. They do so, without the constant stress of tests or teaching to the test.

You may be using a developmentally appropriate mastery learning model. There you would be teaching general knowledge to all of your children together and teaching skills, one-on-one, at their speed.

If you are not using an Age-Grade model, know that you do

not need to know how your children rank against other US children. Why? For the simple reason that your goal is a trajectory of progress on the continuum of learning, not comparison during the learning years.

If your child is moving at their pace and progressing, then there is no need to compare them with other children. What you need to understand is that learning is a continuum.

During a National Emergency, such as with the recent COVID Pandemic, most states temporarily changed their testing requirements. So, it is good to check your state's current testing laws.

HOW DO THEY GET CREDIT FOR THEIR WORK COMPLETED?

For all of the schooling done before high school, it does not matter if the institution is accredited or not. Employment applications usually ask if you finished high school and how much college you have completed. They usually do not ask about studies before high school. So, receiving credit for work before high school is mostly irrelevant.

Employers of non-skilled labor, generally do not send for high school records or college transcripts, or ask if they were accredited.

When applying to college, they do not ask for elementary and junior high school transcripts. They want to know what the student has studied in high school. This can be done with a homeschool transcript and a portfolio.

In our first book-- *A Beginner's Guide to Homeschooling* we talked about the importance of naming and branding your homeschool. We talked about how that comes into play when making official documents like transcripts.

It is important to note that a homeschool diploma is legal in all fifty states because homeschooling is legal in all fifty states.

One way to be credited for work done in homeschool is by exam. In our state of Utah, taking the GED can secure a state issued diploma.

If high school level and college level work has been completed through accredited institutions, colleges and universities usually want to see that transcript.

Many universities base their admissions on the student's ACT score. So, many homeschooled high schoolers will take a practice test to discover their areas they need to work on. Then they will work on those areas and retest. When they feel confident, they take the real test.

Some students (homeschooled, public schooled, and private schooled) will take an ACT Prep class. Then they take the ACT.

The nature of the ACT is that it can be taken more than once. Some students only take the exam once. However, many students will take it until they get a score they like. Students then have their preferred ACT score sent to the college of their choice.

While this does not turn homeschool studies into credits, it does lend credence that the student has prepared. Many selective colleges and universities will take students based on their ACT score alone, without a transcript from an accredited institution.

There are some accredited alternative schools that give students credit for learning. Some by tests and other processes. The North Atlantic Regional High School (NAHRS) in Maine, is a regionally accredited private school.

They evaluate and issue credit for high school level learning. They have a process of demonstrating learning for credit. Since they are a private school, you do pay for the credits.

There are a variety of high school curriculum programs available through accredited public and private schools. Some are via an online class. Others through other modes of distance learning.

Another way students get "credit," is through concurrent enrollment. Some high school students concurrently enroll in college and high school.

They take college classes for college credit and receive high school credit for the same courses. These credits are applied to both the high school diploma and a college degree.

IS STATE TESTING AVAILABLE TO HOMESCHOOLERS?

States that require homeschool testing, provide the testing. Many states do it at no cost to families, other states require the parents to shoulder the cost of testing. Again, we would like to remind you that HALF of the states do not require homeschoolers to take tests.

However, most still make those standardized tests available to homeschool families. Some states cover the test costs, others require homeschool families to cover the costs.

2. WHAT IS THE BEST HOMESCHOOL CURRICULUM?

We get this question *a lot*. It is a common thought that if you just have the perfect curriculum, then homeschooling will be easy. While it is true that finding the right curriculum for your family can have a huge impact on your homeschool, it is definitely not the only factor you need to consider.

It is also important to note that what works for one family might not work for yours. So, while there will be many quick to recommend such and such curriculum, as the end all curriculum, perfect for everyone, it is often not the case in reality.

There are many factors that you need to consider before choosing what curriculum to get for your family to use. Factors, such as which educational models, methods or philosophy resonates with you.

You also need to assess where you and your children are, as far as educational needs and foundation, as well as any special needs to be considered. We walk you through all of this in our last book, *A Beginner's Guide for Homeschooling*.

A simple exercise can help you in seeing if a curriculum will be a good fit for your family. Before you buy a curriculum, no matter how impressive it looks. Visualize actually using every aspect of it with your children.

Is it too complex for your children? Is it too complex for you? Are you going to have to heavily modify it to work for your children? Does it require too much busywork? Will you have to buy and oversee multiple (grades) curriculums for your family? Does it require hours of prep work on your side before each lesson? If you answered yes to more than one of these, please think hard before investing.

Many of the best curriculums on the market offer a sample that you can try out with your children. This is a great way to find the right fit without spending a fortune. You can ensure a good fit for your family before buying. Thus, eliminating the major frustration of buyers' remorse caused by a bad fit.

DO CURRICULUMS HAVE TO BE COMPLEX?

Homeschool curriculum does not have to be complex or filled with busy work to be effective. A simple, clear, varied homeschool curriculum can be powerful. Hands-on is preferred to workbooks and busywork.

In a classroom, busywork can serve as a classroom management tool. Busying children at their desk, enables the teacher to work around the classroom with different students. At home, you do not need that. In this book we will show you how!

In homeschooling, while you work one-on-one with one child, your other children can be engaged in interest-led learning, instead of busywork. Then you rotate through your children for one-on-one.

With the mastery model, children learn new concepts and skills, as they are ready. Self-directed, interest-led learning projects and activities can magnify learning. This is more powerful than busy work in honing skills.

Consider busywork, a parent trap to avoid. Busywork is not an efficient way to learn.

When children are ready for what they are learning, they need less practice to learn. When skills become tools, to help them follow their interest, skills are reinforced, without busywork.

ARE ALL CURRICULUMS EXPENSIVE?

Homeschool curriculum does not need to be expensive, but it certainly can be. **It is important to note that expensive does not necessarily mean better.**

Hardbound, Age-Grade divided curriculum, with workbooks and associated resources, can often get quite expensive.

Printing hardbound books are expensive and having books for each subject and grade can add up. Especially if you have to get a different curriculum for each child.
.

Using an all-in-one curriculum, teaching your family together, and using a mastery approach to teach skills, tends to cost far less than Age-Grade based curriculum.

They also can take less time to implement and be more effective, which is something to consider.

DO I HAVE TO BUY A SEPARATE CURRICULUM FOR EACH CHILD?

In book one, *A Beginner's Guide For Homeschooling*, we talked about the three models of education:

1. Self directed learning

2. Non-Age-Grade Model. This is developmentally appropriate and includes mastery learning.

3. Age-Grade Model. Most public and private schools use this model, it allows one teacher to teach a lot of students.

With the Age-Grade model, yes, you need a curriculum for each child that is in a different grade.

If you use the Non-Age Grade model, it is usually accomplished in one-room schoolhouse style. General knowledge is taught to everyone together.

Teaching all children together can cut down on the expense and time. Skills are taught mastery approach, so it is a text that teaches the subject as a continuum from beginning to end. This can be used for multiple children at their speed one-on-one, at the same time.

While there are some free options for all-in-one curriculum and curriculum split by grade level on line, many one-room-schoolhouse approach curriculums are affordable.

Many one-room schoolhouse curriculums, such as Power of an Hour, are very affordable, to use to teach ALL your children.

One can also get a decent education with just a library card. Most libraries have computer access too. So, even if you do not have computer access at home, they have computers and access for the public to use.

If you have a computer and computer access at home, there are a lot of curriculum helps on the internet, and also free Youtube tutorials and documentaries.

HOW DO I SUPPORT MY CHILDREN'S SUCCESS AND INTERESTS IN THEIR SCHOOLING IN A WAY THAT STILL MEETS STATE STANDARDS?

Most states that have general guideline requirements, mention Language Arts, Math, Geography, Library Skills, Science, History, and so forth. They usually do not specify a list of specific mastery requirements within those subjects, what the exact content has to be, how often to teach a subject, nor how long each day to spend on a subject.

Check your state law. Read it carefully. Does it mention subjects or specify content?

When we see these subjects mentioned, many think of grabbing a workbook and ordering curriculum. It does not have to be that way. You can still include the subjects, but in a different way.

Start with your children's interest and take a project approach. That way they learn subjects within the context of interest led projects.

Perhaps a child had dinosaurs on his mind. You could ask them to write a book on dinosaurs, create a display or presentation. In the process of doing so, they could read about dinosaurs. Reading is a Language Art. They could take notes.

Note taking is a Language Art (library skill and writing). They can do a timeline and show when dinosaurs lived. The timeline uses both History and also Math. Drawing pictures of dinosaurs and labeling the parts, would be both Art and

Science. The student could also diagram the world and show where each kind of dinosaur was discovered. That is Geography.

A PROJECT BASED STUDY EXAMPLE BY DONNA

What if your child wants to learn to cook noodles? Have them read the recipe (Language Arts) and gather the ingredients, then start. I had a child who asked to do this. I handed her the recipe and told her to read the recipe before starting.

Ok, it was actually Julia… Well, she read the ingredients, dumped them into the bowl and nothing stuck together. Ingredients for noodles are cheap, so I said," Did you read the recipe? Try again." She said she had read the ingredients. I suggested she remember my instructions to read the recipe. (Reading) So, she began to gather the ingredients again.

She began to read the recipe and all the sudden, she was measuring (Math) and dumping into the bowl. This time she had followed one instruction on the recipe. Ingredients stuck together a little more, but still not noodles. I asked, "Did you read the recipe?" She responded, "I read until I got to my mistake!" I said, "That was a mistake, go back and try again."

The third time she read the whole recipe. She measured and mixed things according to the recipe and the noodles were fine. She was learning the science of noodles. We talked about how noodles originated in China.(Geography) and how Marco Polo had introduced them to Europe.(History). When a new recipe is mastered, have them write it in their own notebook. (Writing). Notice the subjects were learned naturally, within the context of their interests.

Julia - *I can tell you one thing, I never forgot the lessons I learned the day that I made noodles for the first time. Now, I am not only an accomplished cook, but I know the importance of paying attention to details, reading instructions ALL the way through, and that learning about one topic, will always lead to more.*

HOW DO YOU TEACH CORE SUBJECTS WITHOUT USING LOTS OF WORKSHEETS?

At one time, children wrote their work on a clay or wax tablet. Later, they did their work on a slate or the chalkboard. Much later, they did their work on paper. During the last century, when civilization moved to mass schooling, workbooks and handouts krept in.

It was thought that these pre-printed materials would make life easier on the teachers. **Some refer to this as busywork**.

Why? Because it worked as a classroom management device in keeping children busy, while the teacher corrected papers or worked around the classroom. Those schooled at the end of the 20th century and the beginning of the 21st century likely have experienced this.

Parent groups seeking more rigor in schools have driven more homework and caused teachers to rely more on this busywork paper trail. Our schools, in the last century, moved to dividing children by age and grade, because they wanted everyone to graduate into adult life at eighteen years-old.

This creates many problems within the classroom. Children do not develop by age and there is a wide range of development at each age. This means that same-aged children, in the same classroom, being taught the same things, will be ready to learn different skills at different ages.

Advanced students tend to finish quicker and are often given busywork to occupy them. Always doing busywork for things they already understand can create a closed mindset. They spend most of their school time relearning things they already know. When they come to something new, they may feel apprehensive and think that because they do not already know it they cannot do it. Do they need that busywork? They are ready to move forward.

What about the child who is in the class, but for some reason was not developmentally ready for the concept? They are always being pushed to do work that they are not ready for, which can create a closed mindset. "I am stupid, I cannot learn." Will it help them to be working on doing busywork they are not yet ready to learn?

We have opted for teaching our children at their pace, teaching them together for general knowledge and teaching them individually for skills.

LEARNING AND TESTING THROUGH DISCUSSION AND QUESTIONS

General knowledge can be taught to all of your children together. Each session we begin with a review by asking questions. We ask a question and let them answer. We want them to think. Knowing they will be asked questions and that they will be able to share their knowledge, encourages them to pay attention when we teach. This is a form of test without even having to create and grade a test! Some of these questions can be asked each day, or, if your children are game, all of them.

Questions appropriate to Power of an Hour--

- Who is the person of faith we studied this week? How

did they show their faith?

- Can you recite the Bible Verse of the Week? What does it mean?

- Can you recite the Quote of the Week? What does this quote mean to you?

- What is the Character Theme of the Week? What does it mean? Why is this character trait important to develop or avoid?

- Who is the Artist of the Month? Can you tell me something interesting about the artist? Can you name the Artwork of the Week? Describe it to me. What is the Art Term of the Week? What does it mean?

- What was the Spelling Rule of the Week? Can you give me an example?

- Who is the Musician of the Month? Can you tell me about the musician? What musical piece did we listen to? How did the music make you feel? Can you hum some of it to me, or pick it out on the piano? What is the Musical Term of the Week? What does it mean?

- What is the Grammar Rule of the Week? Can you give me an example?

- Who was the Mathematician/Scientist of the Week? What did you find interesting about this person? What was the Science or Math Concept of the Week? Can you demonstrate it on the white board?

- Who is the World Leader of the Week? Tell me about this person?

- What is the Nation of the Week? Can you show me on the world map? Tell me something about the country?

- What is the Hebrew/Greek letter of the week? What is its literal meaning? Symbolic meaning? Numeric value? Can you write it on the white board?

- What is the Anglo-Saxon/Latin/Greek Root Word or Affix Of the Week? What does it mean? Can you give me an example of a word based on that root or affix?

- Who is the Poet of the Month? What can you tell me about this poet? Can you name the Poem of the Week? Can you recite a portion of the poem? What is the Poetry Term of the Week? What does it mean?

- What is the State of the Week? Can you locate it on a map? What can you tell me about the state?

- What is the Geography Term of the Week?

Before we present new people, events, or concepts, we start by asking them what they already know about the new topic.

- What do you know about Carravagio?

- Can you explain what chiaroscuro is?

- Can you point it out on a painting?

- Can you multiply three digits?

- Will you demonstrate on the white board for us?

- What do you know about Lebanon?

- Can you locate Lebanon on the world map?

Children tend to inhale information. They hear it on the news, read it in a story, discover it on a map. Giving them the opportunity to share what they know, switches them from an "I already know that attitude," to a teaching and sharing attitude.

This is a way for them to learn how to articulate their thoughts and share what they know. Again, a no paper or pencil test and no paper to grade. Sometimes they are eager and their information is incorrect. I acknowledge the information that is correct and then I fill in holes and share further.

LANGUAGE ARTS

Language Arts include all those arts that are used in communication, such as listening, reading, speaking, viewing, visual representation, and writing, as well as sub skills needed for these. For instance, writing includes sub skills such as oral narration, organizing thoughts, penmanship, spelling, grammar, and composition skills.

For some things, we did flash cards. Children should have a hand in making their own learning tools by making their own flash cards. Learning tools do not need to be expensive to work well.

But it is important for children to know they can make their own. It is not always convenient to run to the store or spend hours searching on the internet, only to find out the flash cards they need do not exist.

READING

What is the single greatest predictor of school success? More than affluence, more than race, more than meals together, it is whether the child was read aloud to.

We have had children who taught themselves how to read and children who were taught to read. Before they could read and even after they could read, we would read aloud to our children from rich literature. We started with richly illustrated picture books with prose, such as *Animalia* by Grahame Base and books by Ruth Heller, such as *The Reason for a Flower,* or *A Cache of Jewels.*

I also read aloud other works such as *The Little House on the Prairie* series, *Robin Hood, Childhood Biographies of Famous Americans, Little Britches: My Father and I Were Ranchers, The Princess Academy, Benjamin West and His Cat Grimalkin, From the Mixed-up Files of Mrs. Basil E. Frankweiler, and Laddie: A True Blue Story.*

We had scripture study daily. On top of the King James Bible's moral and literary merit, family scripture study can build high-level reading skills. The King James Bible is written at the twelfth-grade reading level. The scriptures also build vocabulary. Everyone took part. We would sing a hymn, pray, and then read through a chapter. Each person got a chance to read.

Non-readers lap read, one verse with mom. I would run my finger under the words as I read them, they would watch and repeat. Those who could read got to read five verses, with assistance when reading difficulty arose. Over time, the non readers would begin reading and were ready for reading lessons.

How Donna Taught Reading

I personally used Teach Your Child to Read in 100 Easy Lessons to teach my younger four. We went at their pace. That meant on great days we would do a whole lesson. However, on other days we would work through a portion of the lesson, doing a few sub skills. Some days they got scripture study and read aloud, but were not open for a reading lesson. The following day we would resume where we left off.

How Julia Taught Reading

I used the Reading Dynamics (4 Weeks to Read) program with my children. I love how the program is developmentally friendly and incorporates music, flash cards, and activities in the lessons, which were only ten minutes, every other day. It also came with a library of books, which were introduced starting after lesson eight, with new books after every new letter learned. So, my children could gain confidence reading, even before they were done with the program.

Whichever reading instruction method you choose, once children can read, they should be encouraged to have three kinds of reading experiences each day, because these experiences build different skills.

The Three Daily Reading Experiences that Reading Children Need

1. They should be read aloud to.

2. They should have the opportunity to read aloud.

3. They should read silently each day.

Yes, even after they know how to read, reading aloud to them can build knowledge and vocabulary development. Even when they are older, it is important to hear them read aloud. Many children skip words that make them sound out. Reading aloud assures they are learning to tackle those words head on. Reading aloud and reading silently are two different skills.

People usually read faster silently than they can aloud. Children should be encouraged to follow their interests and read silently, then share what they are learning.

Donna's Use of Audio Books

Audio books are also great. We have both utilized audio books in helping our children get on the path to reading. I have two sons that got their reading speed up by following along in a real book, while listening to an audio book. I had a daughter that wanted her own copy of the books I read aloud from. She followed along in her book, as I read aloud. Then when we got in the car, she wanted to read aloud to us, because she just wanted to know what's next.

Julia's Use of Audio Books

I had a daughter who had learned how to read, but wasn't really much into reading. Then her aunt introduced her to the audio books of a fun fantasy series. After listening to the books, my daughter begged me to buy the physical books for her private collection. She promised to read them if I got them for her. I did and she followed through and read them all. Around this time, I started reading another series aloud in the evening to my children, who all LOVED it. Listening to me read the series out loud inspired my son to want to read them himself. So, like his sister I bought the books and he just finished reading them.

A word on getting children to read more, once they can. We have had personal experiences as well as friends and family, of encouraging children to read, by allowing them to stay up after bedtime to do so. Warning, children will push their bedtime, so just set it earlier so they finish at a time you are comfortable with.

Donna's Grandsons and Reading at Night

I have two grandsons who were born 9.5 weeks early and both are high functioning Aspergers. My son, when he was younger, often fell asleep by the light of his clock radio/ That inspired him with his sons. He wanted them to read a certain amount each day, they were reluctant. So, he set bedtime earlier and said they could stay awake an hour, if they were reading. Those boys became voracious readers and often were found asleep with a book in hand at light's out.

WRITING

Writing brings together several skills, as we mentioned above. We believe that for most children, we expect composition too early. We prefer a natural progression from oral composition and penmanship to written composition. Composition writing uses higher level thinking skills. They entail learning the fine art of applying our language conventions of spelling, grammar, and ideas into the written form.

Typically, most children are concrete thinkers in the grade school years. They learn hands-on and through patterns. So, yes, they can learn spelling and grammar facts, because they can learn the patterns and memorize facts. Applying those into a coherent composition, is a skill that often develops in the middle school years.

The British educator, Charlotte Mason, had six year old children learn how to form the letters with beautiful penmanship. Once they could write legibly, she would have them do transcription, or copywork. They hand copied scriptures, poems, lofty inspiring thoughts, and passages from books. This helped the children to become thoroughly familiar with both the spelling of words and the use of punctuation and capitalization.

Children in her school did transcription until they were ten. Then she introduced dictation. She would have a child transcribe a passage several times, thoroughly familiarizing the child with capitalization, spelling, and punctuation. She would then dictate the passage. After they did dictation for a while, by age twelve she had them writing compositions.

Aside from the physical process of learning to write, Charlotte taught spelling and grammar by rule, pattern, and practice over the grade school years.

From the age of six, on, Charlotte Mason had children narrate or tell back a story after one reading. As children grow, a parent can record and type up a narration, then the child can use their own narration for copy work. When on nature walks Charlotte Mason would have children "Picture Paint" with words, a scene they had viewed and were reporting on. She did this to teach them to be honest, not to minimize or to embellish the facts. But this was also a form of oral composition.

When they studied paintings, Charlotte let children spend time observing the art work. Then she would hide the work and have them describe the art work, using detail of color, direction, size, and elements. This too was a form of pre-composition. *I (Donna) used these Charlotte Mason methods with my children.*

So, what is oral composition? It is learning to organize and express your ideas verbally. Little children love Show and Tell, a form of oral composition. Children love to share a story or experience by telling someone else.

Another educator, a Manchester, New Hampshire public school superintendent, Louis Benezet, abolished teaching of grammar, spelling, and composition in the grade school school years, and replaced it with oral composition. Children could report on things they read, were read to them, they heard, observed, or experienced. All grammar, spelling, and composition was taught in seventh grade.

Benezet did this experiment with children from homes where English was not their mother tongue. At the end of his experiment, he brought together the students in the experimental program, with the best students in the capital city of Manchester. The experimental students had years of oral composition and then Language Arts in seventh grade.

The other students had Language Arts throughout grade school and seventh grade. Benezet placed a painting at the front of the class. Children were to write an essay based on describing the painting, as their test.

The teachers did not know who wrote the papers. They graded them and placed them in two stacks. Proudly, the teachers pointed to one stack and said that obviously these were papers from their star students. That pile had richer language and twice as many adjectives as the other.

Upon looking at the papers it was discovered that they were wrong. Those were the papers of the experimental children from homes that did not speak English as their mother tongue. Oral composition during the grade school years, followed by Language Arts in the seventh grade, when brains are mature and ready for it, can yield great results. Benezet's experiment spread and other districts around the United States did the same.

How Donna Taught Writing

I am a journal keeper. My children saw my example. Many of them began keeping a journal, long before formal instruction in writing. They would keep a sheet of paper with the letters to refer to and then ask me how to spell what they wanted to write. Then, I came across a resource I absolutely loved! I loved a specific chapter in the resource. It made the resource worth every penny for me. The book is **Eagle's Wings Comprehensive handbook of Phonics for Spelling, Reading, and Writing** *by Mortimer and Smith,* **specifically Unit 8: Penmanship, Writing, and Book Reports**.

The penmanship teaches print, cursive, and writing numbers. The print has lower case with diagrams that are really easy for children to remember, along with little poems to help them remember how the letter is written, and the direction the letter faces. Then upper case is taught the same way. Then cursive is taught by families of letters that share the same stroke, with their poems too.

*Then there are the **Eagle's Wings 600 Sight Words**. These are 600 of the most frequently used words by children through fifth grade. Words are organized with "like" words and arranged, boxed off from other words: colors, number, time words, be words, opposites, etc. I pulled out the page and had my children lightly color in the boxes with a light hand using color pencils. This makes it easier to find a specific list.*

We stuck this in the back cover of their binder. If they could read, they could find the word and know how to spell it and write in their journal or write their ideas. One day, while I was driving, one daughter caught herself looking up a word the fourth time. She pronounced, "That's it! I am going to memorize this. This is ridiculous. I looked up the same word so many times!"

*Another book I discovered was, **Any Child Can Write** by Harvey Weiner. When I first discovered it in 1988, it was out of print. But I found it in the library. I feel that it was homeschoolers that encouraged this book to be brought back into print. It is a wonderful book about progression in writing from writing lists to writing compositions. It helped me to stop looking at writing as a subject to teach and start looking at it as a tool to learn and use.*

So, I gleaned from Charlotte Mason, Louis Benezet, and Harvey Weiner. My children kept lists, wrote journals, wrote letters, and then I encouraged them to write about their life. I taught them family history and how to research.

They learned library skills naturally, without busywork. Then I encouraged them to start a blog. I knew blogging would bring polish, people will catch errors (and contact them), and it would give my children a voice.

They would learn technology. After starting the blog, they had to watch tutorials and learn how to do things. Some of my children kept their blogs into adulthood and have turned their blogging to a business. But the greatest profit I have seen, has been what blogging has done for their writing.

How Julia Inspires Writing

I am a blogger. I have been running my own website for several years now. My children have often seen me working on a new article. My children will come in and ask what I am writing and I will tell them. Sometimes I'll even read to them excerpts of what I write. I have noticed this in turn, inspiring my children to write, as well, though their work tends to be in the realm of fun, short, fiction tales more often than not.

Additionally, my husband is a talented illustrator, and my daughter takes after him. One day she drew a new character, Derpy the Duck, that she showed my husband. She was so excited she started telling my husband all about her character Derpy.

After listening to her talk about Derpy for over thirty minutes straight, my husband encouraged her to write a book about her character. As she would write, he would then discuss how to improve it with dialogue, descriptions and grammar rules she didn't know yet. So, here my husband took an interest in drawing and turned it into an opportunity to encourage writing.

Going back, when my children were first learning how to write and spell, we did two activities every day, that they really responded to. First, I got the game Bananagrams. Each morning I would spread out the tiles. I would have my children come up with words to describe a theme I chose that morning. I had chosen themes, such as Jesus, gifts, treats, stocking, family time, movies to describe, and what they love about Christmas. If they didn't know how to spell something, they would ask, and I would help them.

The second activity was for writing. I would give them a basic assignment, such as write down what you are most excited about Hallween. Then they would write a paragraph or two full of simple sentences, such as, "I can *not wait to trick or treat. I love candy. I like to dress up. Halloween is fun," about the subject, in their notebooks. These activities were a great starting point to get my kids writing, and the other examples followed.*

MATH & SCIENCE

How Donna Taught Math

Math is the language of science. Yes, math is a language and it is a tool. When I was a young mom, I read the book **Innumeracy: Mathematical Illiteracy and Its Consequences** *by John Allen Paulos. I decided that I needed to use words that prepared them for math.*

I also felt that my children needed to have context to their math. So, I would talk to them about how many place settings we needed for a meal. I helped them learn to read an analog clock with hour, minute, and second hands.

We had a weather thermometer and they learned to read it. We made candy, cooked roasts, learned to make canned food, necessitating them to measure, tell time, and read a cooking thermometer.

I took them grocery shopping with me. I taught them how I made buying decisions on spending our limited cash for necessities. We gardened. We sewed. My children learned math in context as we went. But, I also taught them basic math directly, one-on-one, using the mastery method. We used the mastery method and a white board. They learned basic math first, then after they did it well, they learned to use a calculator.

How Julia Taught Science

For science, I have found that my kids really love watching documentaries, which we then discuss in depth afterwards. There are so many amazingly, well-done, documentaries available to stream online.

We love doing lots of hands-on activities. The other day, I got a quality (made for children) Junior Microscope that can magnify 40, 100, and 400 times. We spent over an hour looking at everyday items closer to see what we could discover. Next time, my son wants to look at germs, and blood cells. At night, we love to look at the stars and talk about astronomy.

We also love to do fun little experiments in our kitchen, to see how things react and work together. When my children are having fun and engaged in what we are doing, they retain so much more, than if I am just having them learn and record dry facts.

When I was growing up, my mother, Donna, learned about nature walks and notebooks from studying Charlotte Mason. So, we went and explored the natural world around us. I loved it so much that I do it with my children, as well. This is often a starting point to many natural science lessons in our home.

HISTORY & GEOGRAPHY

Studying the Bible, great literature, and family history are great segues into studying both History and Geography. As children study these things, they cannot not help but to learn History and become familiar with Geography.

How Donna Taught History and Geography

As mentioned before, I placed a map of the world on our dining room table and protected it with a layer of clear medium weight vinyl. When reading scripture, studying literature, reading history or family history, if they read about a location, the map is there to help us find the location. This has been very handy.

While studying family history, we find out about the events taking place in the world, at that time. I also wanted my children to see themselves as part of history.

At one time, when Julia was young, we had a timeline near the ceiling of *our dining room. It was the only place I could put it, we simply lacked wall space. Then, inspired by Charlotte Mason, I created my own **Book of Centuries**, a timeline in a book. Charlotte Mason's was a single timeline. I decided to have our **Book of Centuries** reflect what was going on in the world on different continents, at the same time. A timeline in a book is a way for a child to take the history they are learning and write about the people and events they are learning.*

*When I was in sixth grade my favorite subject was social studies, which combined History and Geography. We were studying the world. It was hands-on and all of the students got to pick what they wanted to study, then come back and report. I wanted to bring this hands-on into our homeschool. Inspired by the **Book of Centuries** idea, I designed a **Book of Nations**. When we study nations and states, we can create pages about those places and build our own resource book.*

How Julia Taught Geography

A great way to just learn the "facts" of geography is through games! A favorite website that I, Julia, used in college, and now use with my children to memorize the map is https://www.sheppardsoftware.com/. They have lots of fun interactive games that are totally free. Their games make learning Geography easy.

When we started studying more about US Geography I had my husband design some great worksheets that the children used to fill in information about each state as they researched about them. (I share these US Geography printables for free on my site. httpsTheQuietGrove.com)

What about organizing History? Some people use "hook dates" of major world events that helped form Western Civilization. Then you learn about events that led up to those important dates and the results of those events. Why Western Civilization? Because, Western Civilization is the foundation of our American cultural heritage. Also, the ideas and events of Western Civilization, created the country that brought a new form of government, and helped more people out of poverty, than any nation in history.

Another way to look at History, is the Cycles of History. In the book, *The Fourth Turning: An American Prophecy* by Strauss and Howe, the authors show the results of research showing recurring patterns in history. That pattern repeats the cycle every 80 to 100 years, and has a pattern of four distinct phases.

Once, I, Donna, taught a class on college prep. I used this book to help my daughter and other students, to understand the cycles of history, and how it could help them order history in their minds.

Over the last couple years I, Julia, have traveled to many amazing places across the United States and in Europe, with my family. As we travel, my husband and I have made it a point to teach our children about the places we visit. We also like to make sure to schedule stops to museums and historical spots, in the areas we visit. This has been a great way for us to teach our children about history and geography, as well in a very real way, just as my parents taught me.

For example, when we were living in Greece, we took the time to visit Athens and see Zeus's Sky Temple, The Parthenon, & The Acropolis. We also spent a week in Kalambaka visiting the Monasteries of Meteora. While there, we also arranged for a cooking class at a Greek restaurant for our children to learn how to make traditional Greek meals.

We discussed Greek Mythology and history while we were there. Though our children were young at this time, they still remember visiting those places and the things they learned. They are quick to tell you all about it if the topic of Greece comes up.

Recently, while reading the Percy Jackson series to my children, they were so excited when places they had visited and learned about were mentioned in the books.

WHAT DO I NEED TO TEACH MY PRESCHOOLER?

We discuss this in more depth in *A Beginner's Guide for Homeschooling*, but will touch on it here.

While most states promote preschool, no state currently requires pre-school. That's right, It is not necessary to attend preschool. Nor do you need to do preschool at home, for a child to do well in learning in the grade school years.

Children this age need to be focused on learning values, executive function development, physical development, building relationships, and healthy living. These kinds of things are developed hands on, in context, through the home culture, physical play, imaginative play, habit training, family work, family worship, and family service. At this age, children learn better from context, than from curriculum.

Converse with your preschooler. Ask your child questions. Listen to their answers. Use descriptive words (adjectives), such as colors, numbers, quantity, texture, and size. Children develop verbally, more from conversation than from studying Language Arts.

Preschool aged children will gain more from self-directed play at the park, than from being on a sports team. Playing on the play equipment, in the yard or at the park, will help them integrate their senses, build attention span, brain-body balance, executive functions and more.

At this age, the brain develops through the senses. Self-directed play helps them to develop their executive function. This rough and tumble play is just what they need.

3. WILL HOMESCHOOLING AFFECT MY CHILD'S SOCIAL DEVELOPMENT?

When it comes to homeschooling, sooner or later the concern about social development always comes up. I can't tell you how many times friends, family or strangers have voiced the concern to me and other homeschoolers, that homeschooling will harm our children socially.

We seem to think, as a society, that the only way to develop social skills is to isolate our children into groups of other children their own age for long periods of time.

However, I ask you, how often, in the real world, do you find yourself working and socializing only with people your own age?

I don't know about you, but most of my friends are several years older or younger than me. This was also the case, when I worked outside the home.

In the homeschool environment, your children are not artificially isolated in a group of same aged children.

Rather, homeschool children have to interact every day with their siblings who are all different ages, as well as their parents.

Additionally, as they get out to meet with other homeschool families, go to the library, museums, and other places, in the course of their homeschool day, they associate with a wide range of people of various ages.

So, we would contend that, YES, homeschooling will affect your child's social development, only in a more positive way, that better prepares them for real life.

WILL MY CHILD BE SOCIALLY INEPT BECAUSE OF BEING HOMESCHOOLED?

There is a major stigma associated with homeschooling that homeschooled children are always socially inept. A major contributor to this belief, dates back several decades, back when homeschooling was not commonly accepted.

Back then, there were a few extreme homeschool parents, who not only removed their children from public school, but also went as far as to completely isolate their children from ever associating with anyone, not strictly homeschooled.

They didn't want their children to be unduly influenced by public school children. This is a mindset *not* embraced by many homeschool parents today, or then.

In addition to completely isolating their children, many of these parents didn't put a focus on making sure that their children were taught basic social skills, at home. Thus, causing them to be socially awkward and inept, when in public. Even this was rare in its time.

Now we would contend that these children were socially awkward due to their home culture, and would have been socially awkward, even if they had stayed in public school.

However, because they were homeschooled and were under the skeptical microscope of the world. They were put forth as what happens when a child is homeschooled, even though they were only a small subset of homeschoolers.

More recent studies have actually shown that this is NOT the normal outcome of homeschooling. In fact, unless a homeschooled person informed you of the fact that they were homeschooled, you probably wouldn't know (except for how bright they are).

So, unless you are planning on isolating your children and not teaching them any social skills at home, you have nothing to worry about.

WHAT CAN I DO TO HELP MY CHILDREN WITH THEIR SOCIAL DEVELOPMENT?

There are actually a lot of things you can do, and should be doing, to help your children with their social development, no matter where they go to school. A lot of these things deal with your home culture. We go into this in depth, in our last book, *A Beginner's Guide for Homeschooling*. However, we will talk about it a bit here too.

The first thing is teaching your children the core basics of appropriate manners, how to treat others, how to be respectful to elders, how to deal with conflict resolution, etc…

Next, it's important as parents to give your children the opportunity to socially interact with others, both in and outside of the homeschool community.

Here are some ideas for how to help your children be socially active outside of the homeschool sphere:

- Encourage your children to make friends in your neighborhood.

- Invite neighbor family over for dinner (and/or) game nights.

Have regular extended family get-togethers (if you have family that lives nearby).

- Do family service projects in your neighborhood.

- Participate in community events.

These are all activities you can do no matter where you live. Whether there is a large homeschool community or not.

As for social opportunities within the homeschool community, there are several. We go into how to connect with your local homeschool community, and give a long list of ideas, for activities you can do with local homeschoolers, in our book, *A Beginner's Guide for Homeschooling*.

However, here are a few of our favorite activities we have done with other homeschool families.

- Start a book club

- Participate in Park Days & Luncheons

- Enjoy Homeschool Field Trips

- Have a Homeschool Party (these can be especially fun for holidays)

- Put on a fun homeschool play

- Have a Homeschool Spelling Bee or Geography Bee

All of these activities will give your children the opportunity to make friends and connections with other homeschoolers, and provide plenty of social interaction.

WILL MY CHILDREN BE LONELY IF THEY ARE HOMESCHOOLED?

This is a nuanced question. Many children in public schools are lonely, even though they are surrounded by people all day. This is more often a facet of personality vs opportunity.

Personally, this was the case with me (Julia), because I was just very socially shy.

As a homeschool parent, one thing I have noticed is how much closer my children are to each other. My children are each other's best friends. Sure they have friends outside of our family that they love to get together with and video call/chat with. However, their best friends are each other and I am totally ok with that.

If your children are really missing the social environment of school when they start homeschooling, I would recommend doing some of the activities we mentioned in the last section to provide that social interaction they crave.

WHAT DO I DO IF I LIVE IN A SMALL TOWN THAT DOESN'T HAVE OTHER HOMESCHOOLERS?

Socialize with other people in your neighborhood and community. Serve others in your community, with your children. Let your children play with neighbor children, even if they are not homeschooled. Sponsor and event that includes children in your neighborhood.

If you are not far from a larger city, see what homeschool opportunities are available there. Also, consider short day trips into cities nearby. Just be careful, not to schedule during your homeschool time. Also, be wise not to over schedule.

Additionally, consider setting up pen pals with homeschoolers in other states, as well as family who live farther away.

Most of all, enjoy your family culture and do not overlook the socialization that can happen in the home.

4. HOW LONG DO YOU NEED TO SPEND HOMESCHOOLING EACH DAY?

Not as long, as you would think! Studies have shown that even if you taught your children the exact content they would learn in public school, you could get through the work in about 2 hours a day.

Probably, because you are cutting out all the busywork and time lining up to go to other classes, recess and lunch.

When you are teaching younger children it is important to keep your lessons shorter, as well as their official school day.

Why? It has been proven that young minds can only retain so much information, at a given time, before they hit their saturation point. At which point, they aren't learning and retaining information any more, and their cooperation level drops.

We would say that for the younger ages to keep your school day between 2-4 hours.

As your children get older, their school days will get longer, like between 4-6 hours a day, but then more of their study time will be found in personal studies.

DO I NEED TO BE WITH MY CHILDREN OVERSEEING EVERY MOMENT OF THEIR SCHOOL DAY?

No.

OK, let us explain.

Direct teaching should be short, fifteen to twenty minutes a subject. When teaching directly, going at their pace, busywork is not needed.

As they gain skills they should have more time to work on projects of their own interest. This will hone their skills! When they are doing this, you do not need to sit over them. This is not homework. Their interest carries them forward.

WHAT ARE SOME TIPS FOR HOMESCHOOLING WHEN HAVING A SET SCHEDULE IS NEXT TO IMPOSSIBLE?

We would recommend that you structure the time, not content.

Let us explain. At traditional schools and in many homeschool curriculums, you are expected/required to cover a certain amount of content every day. This does not allow for much flexibility or deviation from the structured plan. Because of this, teachers/parents have strict schedules.

However, most kids do not thrive in such an environment. They get frustrated and burned out, feeling as if they are always behind. When this happens, homeschooling becomes a tug of war, with reluctant students and overwhelmed parents.

Instead, we would recommend scheduling blocks of time for any given subject that you can rearrange and fit into your day however works best for you.

For example, I, Julia, have a set amount of time blocks we set aside each day for certain subjects like math, reading, writing etc and we get done what we get done within those time blocks.

Education is not a race where you have to check off having learned a certain amount by a certain time. When you let kids learn at their own pace they are less likely to get burned out. Also by scheduling time blocks (ie we today we will do xx minutes of math, xx minutes of reading, xx minutes of writing…) you can make your actual schedule flexible and fluid to meet your needs.

I, Donna, also did time blocks. Scripture time, Read Aloud time, Gateways. The segments could be done one right after another, or split out during the day. For instance, we did scripture study, followed by read aloud, and then Gateway on most days.

But some days, our schedule was interrupted. We could do scripture study after breakfast, the Gateway at lunch, and the read aloud at bedtime. Also, I could vary the length of the segment. Some scripture stories are longer than others.

Sometimes, they wanted me to finish a chapter in the read aloud, other times they were distracted and I would read a paragraph or two. So, I had segments that could string together but did not have to. I also had each segment flexible to their attention span.

If I was reading, I would pencil in where we stopped and pick up the next day where we left off.

WHAT ARE SOME EXAMPLES OF HOMESCHOOL SCHEDULES?

When it comes to your homeschool schedule, it is important to make one that works for your family. You don't want to just copy someone else's schedule. With that said here are 2 examples of homeschool schedules that we have found works well for our families.

DONNA'S HOMESCHOOL SCHEDULE

My schedule was very easy to remember. My schedule had three parts. I was working with four children, two to eleven when we started this schedule. First, we took a nature walk. That refreshed our minds and invigorated our bodies. Then, I did two one hour blocks a day. The first block had three, twenty-minute segments, and we did it together.

- *General Knowledge Block:*

- *Scripture Study*

- *Read Aloud*

- *Gateway to Learning (General Knowledge Subjects)*

The second hour was the skill development hour, which had four, fifteen-minute segments, and we did these individually.

- *Skill Development Block:*

- *One-on-one for skill learning and mentoring.*

- *Individual self-directed interest-led learning develops skills.*

- *Recess with the youngest, develops executive function.*

I would start the second hour with the youngest child, while the other children had their first block of self directed learning. Then after fifteen minutes, I would place an older child in recess with the youngest, while I worked one-on-one with another child, and one child was getting their second round of self directed learning. By the end of the hour, the youngest had fifteen minutes with each of us, all the older children had two blocks in self-directed learning, and everyone had me for one-on-one, whatever they needed.

JULIA HOMESCHOOL SCHEDULE

Right now, I am homeschooling three young children (ages 6,8,&10). Due to the age of our children, we have kept school simple this last year. I am lucky that both my husband and I work from home, so we BOTH share the responsibility of homeschooling our children.

Our typical homeschool day is from 8 AM - Lunch Monday - Thursday.

We gave the children the option of having shorter days five days a week, or a bit longer four days a week, with Friday free. They unanimously opted for the four day school week, which works well for my husband and I, who both work from home.

We are flexible with the order of our school days, to meet the attention, needs, and schedule of our day. This is what a typical day looks like for us:

We start our school day with:

- *15 Minutes Family Workout/Meditation*

- *45 Minutes Reading*

- *15-20 Writing or Typing (we rotate between the two)*

- *40 Math*

We rotate every other day between:

- *20 minutes Geography (Right now we are focusing on US Geography utilizing printables my husband created for each state.)*

- *20 minutes interest based studies (like creative writing, programming, lego architecture…)*

We end our school day with:

- *45-50 Documentary (We rotate between History, Science, & Geography documentaries)*

- *15-40 Discussion about a documentary and current events.*

LUNCH

*Some days in replacement of the documentary we will do a hands on science project which we discuss afterwards.

Library visits and field trips are usually on Fridays, unless we are meeting up with someone. Then we will adjust that day's schedule.

5. HOW DO I ACTUALLY HOMESCHOOL MY CHILDREN?

This is a question that many new homeschool parents ask. Probably, because there are so many quick to tell you, there is only one right way to do things. However, like parenting, homeschooling is not a one size fits all.

There is no one right, perfect, way to homeschool your children. Not only is every child different, but every homeschool parent is different, as well. You each have different skills, abilities and things to offer.

You also have different personalities, which affect how you teach. For that matter, how you homeschool, also changes, from state to state, depending on the laws and regulations in place. Which is why we walk you through how to set up a successful homeschool, in our last book.

We know this isn't the answer you were probably looking for, but really it's a good thing. Take heart knowing that even though your homeschool may look different, than your friends, or neighbors, it doesn't mean you are doing it wrong.

Thankfully, while homeschooling may look different from home to home, there are certainly common factors that apply to everyone. We discuss these common factors in this and our other books in the series.

WHAT DO I DO IF I DON'T HAVE SPACE FOR AN ACTUAL CLASSROOM IN MY HOME?

This is another thing we cover in our book, *A Beginner's Guide for Homeschooling.* Many parents have the idea that when you set up the "school" part of your homeschool, it needs to look like an actual classroom.

While we have seen some very elaborate and cute homeschool "classrooms," that people have shared on social media, it is really not necessary to have such a set up, to have a successful homeschool.

Personally, we both prefer NOT to have a homeschool classroom. We do our main homeschool work in both our living room and dining room. When school is done and cleaned up we have an actual HOME to live in.

In our living room we have couches, a family computer & printer on a desk and a bookshelf (which has books, homeschool resources, craft items and toys in baskets)

Our kitchen table is large to fit our family and is near a plug socket, back door and sink.

Between these two rooms, we have everything we need for our basic homeschooling days. We just pull out what we need for the day and put it away afterwards.

Since we have more than one child who uses a computer, for some lessons we put one child on the family computer in the living room. The others are on laptops, on the kitchen table. When we watch a documentary, we use the computer in the living room. Then afterwards, we sit on the couch to discuss what we learned.

Our kitchen table is where we do arts, crafts, write papers, and also, sit for discussions. When we were growing up, we had a map on our kitchen table, under a clear vinyl tablecloth. We used this map so often for lessons, as well as family discussions.

When we wanted a nicer table setting, we just covered the map with a cloth tablecloth. This map on our table was the closest we got to an actual classroom, in our home, and we preferred it that way.

There are lots of things you can do to create an atmosphere of learning in your home, without having to make your home look like an actual classroom. We discuss these ideas in our other book.

HOW DO I HOMESCHOOL SEVERAL CHILDREN OF DIFFERENT AGES?

When you focus on mastery level, rather than grade levels, you will often find that your children are closer together in what they should be learning than you would expect.

Also general subjects are easy to teach together for they require no prerequisite of information to learn. This is why we both have done general subjects together with our children, then broken out into one- on-one for skill development.

HOW DONNA HOMESCHOOLED

For me, I homeschooled my younger four children together, for general knowledge. During breakfast, I talked about current events with my children. I took a nature walk together with my children, before we started into school.

Then we did our General Knowledge Block. I read and discussed scriptures with them.

Then I read aloud to all of our children. I taught them, as a group, the following Gateways: People of Faith, Character Theme through the Classics, Art History, Art Appreciation, Spelling, Music History, Music Appreciation, Grammar, Math History, Science History, Math Concepts, Science Concepts, World Leaders, Nations of the World, Language Arts - Roots & Affixes, Poetry History, Poetry Appreciation, and US Geography.

Then we did segments for the Skill Development Block. Each child had one-on-one with me for mentoring and to teach them skills, independent self-directed learning for skill development, and recess for executive function development.

HOW JULIA HOMESCHOOLED

I am lucky to be able to homeschool my children, together with my husband. So, we are able to tag team homeschooling between our three children.

Our youngest joins in on the general subjects, then plays while we work on the subjects that are above him, such as math.

Then my husband and I are able to split our attention between our two older children for those subjects.

WHAT DO I DO WITH MY PRESCHOOLER WHILE I HOMESCHOOL?

Many homeschool moms struggle with knowing what to do with preschoolers who aren't yet in school while they homeschool their older children.

We would suggest letting your preschooler snuggle next to you, as you teach your older children general knowledge subjects.

You can also let your preschooler draw or build with legos at your feet, as you teach. The term preschooler here, means any child under compulsory school age in your state.

After teaching general subjects, while your older children move into their independent self-directed study time, consider taking the time to play with your preschooler. They are the least patient and this makes them happy. If you have more than one child under school age, play with them together.

Then you can place an older child with the preschooler(s), to continue play, while you work one-on-one with another older child, tutoring them in skills or mentoring them. Any other children can continue in self-directed learning. About every 15 to 20 minutes, change the order.

See the following charts.

HERE IS HOW IT LOOKS WITH ONE PARENT, THREE GRADE-SCHOOLERS AND A PRESCHOOLER(S):

Round One (15-20 Minutes)
Mom is with the preschooler(s), whatever the child needs, reading to them, building forts, playing games, etc.

All other children are in self-directed, interest-led study, projects, or activities.

Round Two (15-20 Minutes)
Mom doing one-on-one with Child #1- tutoring skills, mentoring, whatever they need.

Child #3 with preschooler(s) continuing doing play, building, drawing, reading aloud, etc.

Child #2 in the second round of self-directed, interest-led study, projects, or activities.

Round Three (15-20 Minutes)
Mom doing one-on-one with Child #2- tutoring skills, mentoring, whatever they need.

Child #1 with preschooler(s) continuing doing play, building, drawing, reading aloud, etc.

Child #3 in the second round of self-directed, interest-led study, projects, or activities.

Round Four (15-20 Minutes)
Mom doing one-on-one with Child #3 tutoring skills, mentoring, whatever they need.

Child #2 with preschooler(s) continuing doing play, building, drawing, reading aloud, etc.

Child #1 in the second round of self-directed, interest-led study, projects, or activities.

As you can see, it is possible for every child to have one-on-one time with mom, including the preschooler(s). This way each child can have an opportunity to learn new skills at their pace.

Also, the preschooler(s) gets mom first and can also be happy to spend time with each older sibling. Each older child can be happy to play and have the mental break during the school day. Just as important as learning new skills is the opportunity to pursue interests and polish those skills.

Each school age child has twice the amount of time in self-directed, interest-led studies, as they spend in learning new skills.

HERE IS HOW IT LOOKS WITH ONE MOM, TWO GRADE-SCHOOLERS, AND A PRESCHOOLER(S):

Round One (15-20 Minutes)
Mom is with the preschooler(s), whatever the child needs. Read to them. Build forts. Play games.

All other children are in self-directed, interest-led study, projects, or activities.

Round Two (15-20 Minutes)
Mom doing one-on-one with Child #1- tutoring skills,

mentoring, whatever they need.

Child #2 with preschooler(s) continuing doing play, building, drawing, reading aloud, etc.

Round Three (15-20 Minutes)
Mom doing one-on-one with Child #2- tutoring skills, mentoring, whatever they need.

Child #1 with preschooler(s) continuing doing play, building, drawing, reading aloud, etc.

Round Four (15-20 Minutes)
Mom is with the preschooler(s) again, whatever the child needs. Read to them. Build forts. Play games.

All other children are in the second round of self-directed, interest-led study, projects, or activities.

HERE IS HOW IT LOOKS WITH ONE MOM, ONE GRADE-SCHOOLER AND A PRESCHOOLER(S):

Notice, second and third rounds are done during Quiet Time. This way, the preschoolers do not have to have someone playing with them, the older child gets their learning time, and all get Quiet Time, preschoolers get the full 90 minutes and the school age child and mom both get 50-60 minutes.

Round One (15-20 Minutes)
Mom is with the preschooler(s), whatever the child needs. Read to them. Build forts. Play games.

Older child is in self-directed, interest-led study, projects, or activities.

Round Two (15-20 Minutes)
Mom doing one-on-one with older child- tutoring skills, mentoring, whatever they need.

Preschooler is in Quiet Time.

Round Three (15-20 Minutes)
The older child gets a second round of self directed learning. Preschooler is in Quiet Time.

JULIA TWO ADULTS, TWO GRADE-SCHOOLERS, AND A TODDLER

Depending on the subject, either one parent would play with/ work with the preschooler while the other parent worked with the older two children.

Or

Our Preschooler would play nearby while each adult worked one-on-one with an older child.

HOW DO YOU HOMESCHOOL A CHILD WHO HAS LEARNING DISABILITIES

Yes, there are real learning disabilities that children do suffer from. However, many children who are labeled as slow to learn subjects, don't really have disabilities. Rather, they are just not as fast learning a given subject than their peers.

Often this can be because they are pushed into trying to master a subject they aren't developmentally ready for, even if they are generally very bright. They need to be taught in a different way for it to make sense to them. They need more one-on-one attention. Or they are not as interested in the subject.

For children who do have learning disabilities, such as dyslexia, speech impediments, dysgraphia, and dyscalculia, there are some great resources available online, to walk you through tips and ideas, for how to best approach teaching your children.

DONNA ON WORKING WITH ADHD AND HIGH FUNCTIONING ASPERGERS STUDENTS

I have taught students with ADHD and High Functioning Aspergers, in my home, alongside my own children. It is doable, it just takes patience.

First*, make the time as safe as possible, by going at their pace. When they do not feel safe, they shift to fight or flight mode, or survival mode. This is not a teaching place.*

Second*, keep lessons short. Be willing to switch to something else if your* *child shows signs of shutting down.*

Third, *focus on their strengths and interests, for this will keep your child engaged.*

Fourth, *work for steady progress, at their pace. Avoid pushing too far, too fast.*

HOW DO YOU GET YOUR CHILDREN TO FOCUS AND PAY ATTENTION TO YOUR LESSONS?

Remember, children's attention span is about their age in minutes. So, for a six year old, that would be six minutes. A little longer if they are deeply interested, and longer still, if with others showing interest. Less, if they are not interested or merely complying.

So keep lessons short, fifteen to twenty minutes. Be willing to stop and mark your place, if they are beginning to lose attention. Also, be willing to go longer, if they get really engaged.

Other factors that can influence attention and focus are the food they eat, the quality of their sleep, if they are getting enough exercise, and their executive function development.

We have both learned that getting children moving physically, through exercise, or a walk, can help the children focus and pay attention better.

WHAT DO YOU DO WITH A CHILD THAT GETS BORED EASILY WITH SUBJECTS?

The first thing you need to do, if your child is getting "bored" or checking out during subjects, is to determine the cause of the boredom.

- Are they bored, because they aren't interested in the subject?

- Are they bored, because they aren't ready for the subject and it is too much for them?

- Are they bored, because how you are teaching the subject is boring?

- Are they bored, because they already know the information and are impatient to move on?

- Are they bored, because they are distracted?

Knowing the cause of your child's boredom, will help you to easily know how to fix the problem.

If your child is getting bored, because they aren't interested in the subject, consider doing that subject first thing, shortening the time spent on it each day, or even tabeling that subject for a short while.

If your child is getting bored, because they aren't ready for that subject yet, and it is over their head, consider taking a step back to make sure the foundation is there first, and then not move forward, until the child is ready.

If your child is getting bored, because you aren't teaching in an engaging way, or a way in which they process information, then try switching it up, and make sure you are not checking-out yourself on that subject.

If your child is getting bored because they already know the information and are impatient to move on, then consider either giving them assignments to delve deeper into the subject or just let them move on.

If your child is getting bored, because they are distracted by something near them, or something else they want to do? Consider removing that distraction from their life or letting them know if they don't focus, you will do so. We have both had to do this with electronics from time to time, and this is also why we don't create an over stimulating "Classroom" for our children to learn in.

HOW DO I CRISIS SCHOOL?

Breathe.

Crisis school can be anything from mom health issues, child health issues, a move, a local emergency, to a national, or international crisis. You need to stop and know you can do this. Take time to center yourself and assess what you can do.

HOW DONNA DID CRISIS SCHOOLING

I have had hyperemesis gravidarum (severe morning sickness) that put me to bed, with little energy to do much. I was able to read and do general knowledge from my bed. During the worst of it, my older children got more independent self-directed interest-led learning, and I worked with my little boy for a few minutes on reading. I basically had a little over an hour of energy. But they learned and kept moving forward. When I hit my worst part, my dear homeschool friend, Lenore, stepped in and offered to teach my son to read, until I could resume teaching him.

So, you need to take time to assess what you can do. Recently, our whole culture has gone through a world pandemic. That crisis resulted in schools closing. You still would benefit by taking a few days to read and consider the steps we went into depth discussing in *A Beginner's Guide for Homeschooling*.

Consider the following:

1. Write down your why for homeschooling, instead of distance schooling. Create a vision of where you want your homeschooling to lead your family.

2. Assess where you are, your strengths, and areas needing strengthening. Do the same for your family, and also for each child.

3. Create Your MAP - Your Homeschool Business Plan

4. Consider the home routines and family culture. They will change when you are all there 24/7. Simplify,

5. Consider self-care as nonnegotiable. If mom is not taking care of mom, she will burn out. Less is more!

6. Consider a simple record keeping, just one page a day.

Keep it short and simple. Start with daily exercise. Read and discuss scripture. Capture their imagination with reading aloud to them. Then add on to this basic routine, expanding into other areas of knowledge and doing activities that use their skills naturally.

Play games together, build relationships. You can also utilize learning apps and websites to supplement what you are teaching. These educational games can be played by your children, without a lot of oversight.

HOW DO I HELP MY CHILDREN TO LOVE LEARNING?

The most important thing you can do to help your children gain a love of learning, is to show them that YOU love learning. Children watch and learn from watching us. If they see you excited about learning and taking the time to read, and learn new things every day, they will want to do the same.

Next, consider building on your children's interests and strengths. This will keep learning fun, engaging and give your children the confidence to conquer harder things.

Lastly, if you want your children to LOVE learning, then make learning FUN and ENGAGING! If your children are enjoying themselves, they will want to do it more. There is a lot of truth to the old adage, "If you aren't having fun, then you aren't doing it right."

Simply switching up what you are studying, adding hands on elements, and tying the subjects into real life with stories, people and practical application, can do wonders.

6. WHAT DO YOU DO IF YOUR CHILD DOESN'T WANT TO BE HOMESCHOOLED?

We all have our reasons why we have chosen to homeschool our children. Yes, it can get frustrating when one (or more) of our children don't want to be homeschooled. Especially, when they won't cooperate with our sincere efforts. It is easy to fall into the mindset of, "It doesn't matter what you think, you are going to do it anyways!" Sadly, this doesn't often end well for the parent or the child.

Rather than strong-arming your children into compliance, we would recommend sitting down with your children in an open conversation.

This is where you LISTEN to their thoughts, feelings, and concerns. As you do, you will discover exactly why they don't want to homeschool. This will give you a better idea, on how to address their needs.

When your child isn't feeling heard or understood, it can easily transform into demands to go back to public school. Also, it can turn into refusal to do homeschool assignments. This can also result in an overall conflict-ridden relationship, between you and that child.

This doesn't need to be the case. Patiently, listen to your child. Validate what they are thinking and feeling. Do this BEFORE sharing the why behind your decision to homeschool them. This will give you the opening to discuss and address their fears, concerns and needs. They may feel their needs won't be met in the homeschool environment.

WHAT DO YOU DO IF YOUR CHILD ASKS TO GO BACK TO PUBLIC SCHOOL

Again, the first thing you need to do is find out their motivation for that request.

Has your child grown peer dependent? They may not know how to socialize outside a narrowly defined peer group. They may need opportunities to learn from broader social experience. Or they may just need the reassurance, that they are not being cut off from the world, by being homeschooled. They will still have their friends and many opportunities to socialize.

Sometimes, mom is distracted and the child is needing more attention and more interaction with you. In those cases, this can be a wake up call to you. Time to step back and tune out your distractions. Also, time to give your children the focus they need and deserve.

Other times, children look at the back-to-school hoopla. They may feel that they're missing out. They want to ride the bus, have new clothes, a new backpack, or lunch box.

You can still meet the need through homeschool. You can take your children to get a new special outfit or two. Consider buying some fun school supplies for the new school year.

Moms can even do a fun back-to-school party with friends. Take back to school pictures to make the new school year feel special for your children.

It is also a good thing, when dealing with children wanting to go back to public school, to ask yourself, is your family homeschool what you envisioned? What are you NOT doing, that you planned on? Is homeschool, as being done in your home, something you would have enjoyed doing as a child? What can you do to improve this? Often, this assessment will show you areas where you can make homeschooling more enjoyable and effective in your home, for both you and your children.

Consider brainstorming with your children about the benefits they can have, in schooling at home. What would they really like to study and do in your homeschool? Talk to them about their interests. How can you weave that into your homeschool? Talk about their concerns. Are they wanting something from school that they think only school can offer? What are ways those concerns can be met in homeschool? In what ways can those needs be exceeded through homeschool, that cannot be done in school?

Sometimes, you can find alternative options to the classes and extracurriculars in the homeschool or local community, such as homeschool choirs or city league sports. Other times, for older children, it may be an option to do a special partial enrollment. This would allow them to participate in certain classes and extracurriculars, at their local high school.

Julia *When I was homeschooled, I really wanted to participate in some of the plays at the local high school with my friends. I went in with those friends that were in the drama department, to talk to the drama teacher. In doing so, I got special permission to try out for their plays and musicals, even though I was a full time homeschool student.*

My older brother was able to do a partial enrollment, to join the high school acapella choir, and also, to be a part of the track team. There are many options, if you are willing to do the footwork to look.

WHAT DO YOU DO IF YOUR CHILD IS REFUSING TO DO THEIR HOMESCHOOL ASSIGNMENTS?

In the case that your child is refusing to do their homeschool assignments, we would recommend considering approaching your homeschooling in a different way. Homeschool does not need to be treated as domestic chores, doling out of assignments. Think about your end goals. Why are you giving assignments? Are there other ways to achieve those goals?

Often when children are refusing to cooperate there is a disconnect in the parent-child relationship or a disconnect on what they child needs. If you are just coming to homeschool, you may need to take time to heal from difficulties the child had at school, time to build the parent child relationship, time to navigate supportive routines, or time to fall in love with learning again. Also. they may not be ready yet for independent assignments and need more hands on interest led learning.

What are their interests? Is your family homeschool building on your child's interest? Does your child feel their interests are not validated? Consider self-selected self-directed project learning.

Would the child be willing to teach the family or a few families about their interest? Would they be willing to research and write a book about their interest? Would they be willing to create a game to teach their interest to others?

WHAT DO YOU DO WITH A CHILD WHO LOVES TO ARGUE OR ARE DEFIANT ABOUT EVERYTHING?

When a child is very argumentative or defiant, there is often an underlying cause that may not be obvious. Has this child always been this way, or is it something new? When you say they are argumentative and defiant about "everything," what do you mean?

Are they defiant when assigned chores or given school assignments? Do they really argue about everything? Being defiant and argumentative is a clue that you need to nurture their core foundation. This behavior can reveal lack of conflict resolution skills, issues with showing respect, self-regulation issues, impulse control issues, and can be a sign of deeper issues. It is time to gather more information about what is going on with the child. However, underlying health issues can also result in such behavior. Before changing everything:

ASK YOURSELF HOW IS YOUR CHILD'S HEALTH?

Are they acting out because they are hangry? Perhaps the balance of their diet is off, which can totally result in behavior issues. Often, when children and adults eat high carb diets, they get higher insulin levels, and big crashes of blood sugar an hour or two after eating. When the blood sugar drops, many individuals get hungry, impatient, irritable, and angry-- hangry.

Growth spurts can leave a child hungry and irritable.

Sometimes they are missing or deficient in a few key nutrients, such as D3 from sun and magnesium. And, sometimes their gut health is off due to medications, stress, or even chemicals in foods they eat.

Evaluate what your child is eating. Consider taking time to menu plan so you can make sure they are getting a delicious diet that does not cause an insulin spike and provides nutrients they need for good brain function.

How is your child's sleep? Disruptive sleep can make it difficult for children and adults. Sleep issues can leave children, teens, and adults easy to anger. Sleep issues can result in mood issues. The bright light from screens can disrupt the body's serotonin production, melatonin production, and sleep cycles. Before you run out and grab melatonin, it is a hormone, when we take it instead of adjusting lifestyle issues, we can cause our body to make less melatonin. It is good to not let children use screens one to two hours before bedtime. Shut off the screens.

Do they need to take a walk before starting the bedtime routine? Consider working together to tidy the house. The benefit is, floors are clear of obstacles, if there is a night-time emergency, and you get to wake up to a clean house. Then have a peaceful bedtime routine. Spend a few minutes with each child before bedtime. Take time to think of the good things they did that day. Recognize their victories. So, if they are angry and defiant, do what you can to support health sleep habits.

HOW IS YOUR CHILD'S IMAGINATIVE PLAY AND PHYSICAL ACTIVITY?

Children develop their executive function through working together and playing together. It is through work and vigorous play that children learn and develop sensory integration, emotional self-regulation, and impulse control.

Too much sedentary activity, can mean these executive functions do not develop as they should.

As far as play goes, being on a sports team, does not develop the child. as much as self-directed vigorous play. They need to walk, run, crawl, jump, balance, spin, slide, swing, brachiate, sway, climb, and more. Most sports only use a few of these. So, if they are angry and defiant, get them outside more and get them moving more.

CHORE WARS?

Is your child bucking you when you assign them a chore? Parents often resort to punishment and threats to get a child to do assigned tasks, after having tried rewards to entice their children to work. Children can get overwhelmed with many household tasks and may not be ready to work solo.

In our first book, *A Beginner's Guide for Homeschooling,* we discussed at length, training children how to work. Children may know what you want them to do. Children may struggle with executive function development, organizational skills, and where to start.

We suggest you start with habit training. Habit training is not habit telling. It is walking them through that habit until they have that pattern.

Then consider family work. Here they learn the patterns of how to work and develop executive function. Most children do better when led, than they do when they feel manipulated or coerced.

Children often work better with you, than in isolation and alone. When you work with them, they learn how to set the goal, organize a plan, pay attention to detail, follow through, finish, and they learn to go at your pace. These are important nuances that are not taught, but are patterned. So, you might want to consider how work is happening in your home and how to work together.

DOES YOUR CHILD FEEL INVISIBLE?

Many children act up and are defiant because they feel invisible and that they have no power in their lives. If lifestyle issues are fine and you have addressed work, you need more information. Listen to your child. Discover their inner battle. Let your actions show that you listened, are working towards better communications, and better ways in your home. Sometimes, showing care by listening, helps them see that you value them.

WHAT IF YOUR CHILD DEFIES YOU AS THEIR TEACHER?

This is more common than you think. This often happens when parents lose sight of their homeschool vision and resort to recreating their vision of school at home. This can be even more acute when education is reduced to just endless "school work," (busywork) instead of learning.

Education does not need to look like homework. It also does not have to appear as most adults view school. Learning is not a chore on a check off list. If you are handing out lists of assignments and are getting defiance, stop, step back, and assess. What other ways are there to teach your child?

WHAT DO YOU DO IF YOUR CHILD IS BURNT OUT AND SHUTDOWN TO LEARNING?

"Certainly, trying to teach the head while ignoring the body and emotions may account for a great deal of school failure."
— Jane M. Healy, Endangered Minds: Why Children Don't Think And What We Can Do About It

Step back. Take time to heal, build relationships, build self-concept, focus on the victories, and build a love of learning.

Assess health, strengths, and areas needing strengthening.

Address health and lifestyle issues.

Focus on strengths and interests.

Take long walks. Being outdoors is incredibly healing and is also a place that stimulates curiosity. Curiosity drives inquiry. Inquiry drives searching. Searching drives learning.

Read. Read to yourself. Laugh. Respond to what you are reading. This will arouse their curiosity. Read aloud. Read interesting inspiring stories. Let the stories inspire some of the activities you do. Keep reading.

Reading and sharing can drive curiosity. Remember, curiosity drives inquiry. Inquiry drives searching. Searching drives learning. Consider this poem and how reading can awaken the heart to learning.

The Reading Mother by Strickland Gillilan

"I had a mother who read to me
Sagas of pirates who scoured the sea,
Cutlasses clenched in their yellow teeth,
"Blackbirds" stowed in the hold beneath

I had a Mother who read me lays
Of ancient and gallant and golden days;
Stories of Marmion and Ivanhoe,
Which every boy has a right to know.

I had a Mother who read me tales
Of Celert the hound of the hills of Wales,
True to his trust till his tragic death,
Faithfulness blent with his final breath.

I had a Mother who read me the things
That wholesome life to the boy heart brings-
Stories that stir with an upward touch,
Oh, that each mother of boys were such.

You may have tangible wealth untold;
Caskets of jewels and coffers of gold.
Richer than I you can never be —
I had a Mother who read to me."

Play games together. Games have rules. Games use lots of skills and do not seem like school. Games use Math. Some games use Language Arts. Others teach Geography.

Whatever you do, don't let entertainment, edutainment, and a computer screen fill the void and take the front seat. Sure, children need to learn how to use devices. However, at the time they are shut down, is not the time to let screens take the stage, front and center.

Technology has the capacity to stall a child's recovery from burnout and narrow their focus. Take care of the healing. Focus on strengths. Build relationships. Work together. Enjoy the outdoors. Read aloud. Play games together.

WHAT DO YOU DO IF YOU ARE BURNT OUT AS A HOMESCHOOL PARENT?

This is actually quite common in our modern world. The problem is that most of us try to do more than is necessary, resulting in getting overwhelmed. All while, ironically, still feeling as if we aren't doing enough, causing us to do, even more. Then, burnout is the natural outcome.

If this is you, then Stop. Breathe. Assess. Create a vision. Simplify routines. Most of all give yourself grace.

Consider whether your family is engaged in too many activities. You may have to do fewer activities, while you work to bring life into balance. Being pulled by too many activities can be overwhelming. If mom is burned out, the family probably is too. Learn the concept: less is more.

Know that you can say, "NO, not at this time." You do not even have to give an explanation. When you try to excuse yourself, through explanation, it challenges the other person to figure a work around and convince you.

Sometimes, all we can do is stop everything. Take everything off our plate, then only add back the most important things.

- How is your self-care?

- Are you getting beauty sleep? Beauty Sleep is the hours of sleep you get before midnight.

- Do you take time in the morning to pan your day?

- Are you getting enough exercise?

- Is laundry stacking up?

- Is the house mess suffocating you?

- Are meals on time?

Now assess and figure out why things are happening or not happening. Consider reading the chapter on Mom Care in our first book, *A Beginner's Guide for Homeschooling*.

HOW DO YOU AVOID BURNING OUT IN THE FIRST PLACE?

In the first place, you are more likely to not burnout if you have done the following:

1. Know your why and have your vision of homeschool success. When you know why you homeschool and have a vision of success, it is much easier to avoid burnout.

2. Have taken time to assess yourself, your family, and each child's strengths and what needs strengthening? Having this picture in your mind can help you avoid hours of unnecessary frustration, because this helps you have laser focus on what you need to do.

This helps you see, you do not need to do
everything right now, that learning is a continuum.

3. Have You Created Your Homeschool Business Plan? Creating a Homeschool Business plan can help you navigate the hardest days.

4. Have you addressed your home culture foundation? Getting homeculture into place can alleviate a lot of difficulties that can wear a mother down.

5. Do self-care. Ignoring our needs can be a shortcut to burnout. So, make sure you do take care of yourself. If life is so hectic that you have no time to care for you, you will deplete yourself.

6. Keep simple records. Keeping simple records can help us keep perspective.

We address all of these in greater depth in our first book - *A Beginner's Guide for Homeschooling.*

7. WILL HOMESCHOOLING PUT MY CHILDREN BEHIND?

When we hear parents voice their concern that one of their children is behind, our first thought is always, "Behind what?" Their peers? Socially? Academically? Really, there is no such thing as behind. Education is a journey not a race. We all travel at different speeds at different times. This is natural.

We need to remove the concept of "BEHIND" from our mind and vocabulary, because it is not only a false concept, but referring to our children in such terms only causes them to feel like there is something wrong with them. It can cause your children to feel like they are failures, which leads to their confidence dropping, which in turn leads to burn out and full-on shut down.

Research done in states where children are required to test, show that homeschool children on average, outperform their public school peers on standardized achievement tests. Socially, if you did not know which children in a room were homeschooled, you would not be able to pick them out by the social actions.

While different children will take longer with certain subjects than others, they are often faster than those same peers on other subjects. This is natural. Stop worrying about it. Just focus on their strengths. and their weak spots will eventually take care of themselves, as your child gains confidence and a love of learning.

"I wonder how many children "decide" they are dumb about certain subjects, when the truth is that someone simply laid on the learning too soon in a form other than one needed to receive it at the time. Thus they were cheated of the chance to learn it, in an appropriately challenging and satisfying way." Jane M. Healy author of *Endangered Minds: Why Children Don't Think and What We Can Do About It.*

Julia - *Let me tell you a story about when I was nine years-old. At this time, I was in the third-grade, attending public school, and I was two years behind in reading. OK, I was labeled way behind. I could read, but not fast or smooth in reading. I was so halting in my reading out loud that I was painfully embarrassed when required to do so, in front of my class, in group reading. A concern was voiced more than once by my teacher, in front of me, that this would cause me to fail in school and life, if not fixed right away. So, they had me working one-on-one with the reading specialist. But it only made it worse.*

I felt like a complete failure and stupid. Never mind the fact that I was actually labeled gifted when it came to math, all I could see was my weakness that was constantly told to me by my teacher.

When school was out for the summer, unlike my teacher, my parents didn't focus on my "weak spot." Rather, they focused on helping me come to love books. They did this by reading aloud to me from the classics. They also inspired me by including me in grown up discussions of things they were learning from their readings.

Slowly, I began to gain confidence in myself again and decided that I was going to conquer reading. I worked in secret every day with a program my mother had actually bought for my brother. Mom did not even know I was doing this.

By the end of the summer I could read and comprehend anything put in front of me. They tested my class at the beginning of fourth grade to see if we lost reading skill over the summer. I have advanced from two years below grade level to two years above grade level in two months. They thought that was impossible and retested me in October.

By then, I tested three years above grade level across the board along with the other subjects. This led to them having me skip the rest of my fourth grade year and finish the second half of the year as a fifth grader. This was the year before I started homeschooling full time.

*Was it my teacher constantly telling me that I was behind, that helped me to improve my reading? No it wasn't. In fact, it almost caused me to give up on reading altogether. Though I am sure that was not her intention. It was the confidence gained by my family not focusing on my weakness that allowed me, **when I was ready**, to conquer and develop the skill I was lacking.*

And no, being late to develop my reading skills hasn't hindered my education or success at all. To this day, I love reading so much I read 3-5 books on average a week.

Donna - *Later, Julia's next younger sister was struggling with reading. After learning from Julia's experience, I waited and focused on other learning. When she was ready she came to me asking for help, and we tackled it together.*

HOW WILL I KNOW IF THEY'RE ON TRACK WITH CHILDREN THEIR AGE?

Consider the typical public school classroom. Classmates are the same age. They get the same lessons and assignments, for which they are given grades. Then they have the same homework and are graded. The class takes the same tests and are graded. They take the same standardized test. These students are compared to each other and ranked. Then all of them are moved forward together (often even when some are practically failing in their grades).

Some children are developmentally ready and others are not for what is expected of them. When children are taught when they are ready, they learn faster than when we try to hot-house them and teach them when they are not ready.

Children in a typical classroom are not developing along a bell curve. Recently, the National Assessment of Educational Progress showed that by the end of fourth grade only 36% of American children were proficient in reading at grade level or above. That means that 64% of children were reading below grade level proficiency. No state tests proficient. By the end of eight grade, only 32% were reading proficiently, at grade level or above. Remember, typically, home schooled children average above the 80th percentile.

Many children who were functioning poorly in school, were then homeschooled for a time. After homeschooling, they came back to school and were considered advanced students. It is not that homeschoolers are cramming, but it is easier to learn one-on-one and in small groups. Homeschool children have more time to pursue interests.

If children go back to school, after homeschooling, the school does not usually place them according to performance. They are typically placed with age-mates. This is the case, even when children are functioning above their peers or when they are not at grade level.

If they are not at grade level most of their peers are not really at that level either. If you create your vision and homeschool business plan, and are consistent, your children will progress and it is unlikely that they would test below grade level.

HOW DO I ASSESS MY CHILDREN'S LEARNING?

When you are actively involved in your children's learning, you will see when they are understanding concepts and when they need more time on them. This is a day to day thing. When your children are getting it, you move forward. When they aren't grasping a concept yet, it means that you need to take more time on it, or maybe even approach teaching it to your children in a different way.

The first step in assessing your children's learning is assessing what their strengths are. What do they enjoy doing and excel at? Are there areas they are struggling in? Could part of the struggle be that your child is not ready for your expectations? Years ago, kindergarten was play based.

Kindergarten readiness was determined not by whether the child could read, know their colors, write, or count. Readiness was determined by executive function development.

- Can they follow directions?

- Are they self-regulating in their emotions?

- Can they control impulses?

- Do they have coordination?

- Do they have fine motor control? Could they sit still?

Research then, showed that over 60% of boys and many girls were not developmentally ready for kindergarten at age five.

Donna - *I had a son that wanted to do copy work with his older siblings. He was kindergarten age, but we live in a state that does not require kindergarten and I teach at my children's pace. So, I gave him some paper and pencil.*

He was really struggling and I noticed his fingers were not strong enough, yet. So, I let him finish and said, "We do not need to do this right now. Perhaps we will do more writing next fall." He did not mention it again.

Later that spring I came into a room, there he sat, writing beautifully. He was not ready when he wanted to do what the older children were doing, but several months later he was ready and decided to do it.

HOW DO I DEFINE SUCCESS?

Honestly, this is a very personal definition and is different for each person. Really, it ties back into your homeschool why and vision that we talk about in our last book.

Some people define success as getting their children to college and a degree. For others, college has nothing to do with it. They define success as being a happy adult and able to care for themselves and others.

It is important that you define success for yourself and your family and not let others try to define it for you.

On a yearly basis, is success learning and progressing day to day until the end of the school year? Is success completing a textbook? If you finish it early, it is a success.

Then what do you do? You have success. But if you have not decided what success is, you may wonder if you should start the next level book.

What if you do not complete the book during the school year? Do you keep going? Do you wait until the next school year? Was the year you spent and everything learned a failure because you didn't finish everything you set out to?

We use a mastery model. For us, learning is a continuum. We work for consistency and progress in learning. We block time for learning and move at their pace. We strive for variety and understanding. Success each year is consistency in daily progress and arriving at the end of the school year.

We feel that learning is a journey and a continuum, not a destination.

For us the ultimate measure of success is if our children have learned and grown and still have a love of learning.

8. HOW DO I PREPARE MY HIGH SCHOOLER FOR COLLEGE?

This is a topic that is big enough, that we will be covering it in depth in a later book in our Homeschooling Basics series *What You Need to Know About Homeschooling High Schoolers*

However, we do want to make sure we adequately discuss it here to answer these commonly asked homeschool questions to get you started.

We want our high schoolers to develop broad and deep knowledge. We want them to be able to read and understand at the college level, be able to write clearly and persuasively, and have a solid understanding of practical math. But beyond that, the field they want to study may require certain preparation.

Additionally, the college or university they want to attend may have some specific study requirements.

Colleges like to see that a student did more with their life than just study. They like well rounded students that develop talents, serve in the community, and get involved. They want to know that the prospective student will be an asset to their campus.

WILL MY CHILDREN BE ABLE TO GET INTO COLLEGE IF THEY ARE HOMESCHOOLED?

Yes! Many selective top tier colleges and Universities accept homeschooled applicants every year.

It is important to note that just attending high school, earning good grades, and receiving a diploma is not a guarantee for college entrance at a top tier college.

Whether a student attends public, charter, private or homeschool during college, they need to gain the knowledge and skill to qualify for the select universities. Most require a good ACT or SAT Score. And that takes a lot of preparation.

There are also many routes to college that do not require a diploma from an accredited high school.

ACT/SAT

Many students take a prep class for the ACT and still end up taking the test more than once till they get the score they desire. Then they send their best score to the colleges and universities they want to apply to.

Many homeschool and high school students persevere and work hard to learn the subjects tested and learn good test taking strategies. They earn high enough test scores, to not only get into college early, but earn great scholarships, too.

CONCURRENT ENROLLMENT

is taking college classes in high school and receiving both college and high school credit for the same courses. These students graduate from high school and earn an associates degree at the same time.

COMMUNITY COLLEGE AND NON-SELECTIVE STATE COLLEGES AND UNIVERSITIES

Some students enter these schools and get a great education. Others demonstrate they can do college work at the non-selective school and then transfer to the school of their choice to finish their degree.

WHAT DO YOU NEED TO DO TO PREPARE YOUR CHILD TO GET INTO COLLEGE?

This depends on the route to college your youth chooses to take. This also depends on the college or university they want to attend, and the degree they want to pursue.

Contact the university of their choice. Speak to the admissions department and ask for their "Homeschool Specialist."

Not everyone in the admissions department is well versed in the homeschool application process.

Also, if your youth knows what degree they want to seek, it is a good idea to talk with that college within the university, and discover how to best prepare.

DOES MY CHILD NEED TO DO ACCREDITED HIGH SCHOOL CLASSES TO GET INTO COLLEGE?

While it is a common belief that homeschool students need to take accredited classes in high school, to get accepted into colleges and universities, this is simply not the case.

Yes, "if" your child does take accredited classes, then it is important to know that most colleges and universities require these courses to be included in your child's high school transcript.

DOES MY CHILD NEED A GED TO GET INTO COLLEGE?

In some states, passing the GED gets you a state issued high school Diploma. Which is why some students choose to get a GED. They feel more validated by getting it.

Others are confident of their preparation and do not seek a GED, and instead are proud of their homeschool transcript.

The important thing to note is that a GED is not a requirement for most colleges and universities. Especially, if the student applying has good ACT/SAT scores.

HOW DO I CREATE TRANSCRIPTS FOR HOMESCHOOL?

When creating a transcript, it is important that it looks professional. This is why we recommend having an official school name and logo, as we explained in book one on the section about branding your homeschool.

Typically, high school students can take only six classes a semester and if you transcript has more, it may not be taken seriously. Look at your state law to see how many courses of each subject students are required to graduate.

When not taking a class, but studying on their own, you are looking at gaining equivalent knowledge. If a student learns Algebra in half the time, the student still learns Algebra. If it took them longer, they do not have more credit.

If the student either took a college level course or did a Mass Open Online Course (MOOC) which are free college courses online, that course would be listed as honors credit.

Look at your local high school's course names, to get a clear idea of how to name the courses on the transcript, that describe what your child has studied.

HOW DO YOU APPLY FOR COLLEGE AS A HOMESCHOOL STUDENT?

Each college and university has their own process for homeschool students applying.

Check with the university of your choice and find out their process.

Ask for their "homeschool specialist." So many homeschool students have attended college and done well, that many universities have a homeschool tab on their admissions process on line.

9. HOW DO I PREPARE MY HIGH SCHOOLER FOR A CAREER?

Career development begins at home, while your children are young. It begins with gaining a strong work ethic! Again, this goes back to their early training and core foundation. Work with them and help them gain good work habits and attitudes. If you do so now, it will greatly impact their academics and later business success.

As your children grow, consider inviting interesting people into your home, to share dinner with your family and talk about what they do for a living. Their passion will inspire your children to seek their own.

Take field trips and learn about what is involved in different careers.

As children get into high school ages and begin considering possible life paths, consider connecting with people on those paths. Invite them into your home. Let them share about their career.

HOW DO I HELP MY CHILDREN DEVELOP SPECIAL INTERESTS

The most important thing you can do as a parent, to help your children develop special interest, is to become interesting.

Broaden your horizons. As you do, you show your child the way. Children are trying to grow up.

We as the parents are their most important example of what being grown up looks like. So, as we explore, try new things, find new interests and develop them, we show our children how to do so themselves.

This is just as true for young children as it is for High Schoolers.

HOW DO I HELP MY CHILD DISCOVER THEIR PASSION?

Children learn from watching others. If you want your children to seek out, find and develop their passion, you need to do so first. As your children see you embracing your passion, they will be inspired to follow in your footsteps, by embracing theirs.

So how do you help them find their passion? Well passion begins with interest. The more your children are exposed to different people, places, experience, and things the more they will find that sparks their interest. From there passion can grow.

A WARNING:

Too often, as soon as a child expresses interest in anything, parents tend to go overboard by over committing their child.

As an example, a little girl sees a ballerina. She tells her mother she loves ballerinas and wants to be one someday. The mother in excitement goes and signs her four year-old up for a year's worth of classes, buys several leotards, tutus and ballet slippers.

However, after just a few classes the child loses interest. But the mother says, "Too Bad. I spent too much money on this. You said you wanted it. I don't raise quitters. You will stick with it, and practice and be a great ballerina whether you like it or not."

The truth of the matter was, this child just wanted to dress up and pretend to be a ballerina, and was too young for that sort of commitment. Her mother would have been better off, taking her daughter to the ballet, getting her a dress up costume to play and imagine in. And maybe even asking a local dance studio if she could audit a class or two to see if it is really something she wanted before jumping head first and spending a fortune on a child's whim.

When our children express interest in something. Take it step by step. Provide opportunities for them to get a closer look. But don't push them too far, too fast.

If it is to become a passion, it will. If not, the experience will still be to their benefit.

Another thing to consider as you try to help your older children find their passion. When your high schooler shows interest in something, it is important to validate that interest and not just push it aside because it doesn't look like something that we think will be worth a carrier.

Julia - *My husband is a talented artist, but for years was told by many, that his interest in art was nice, but not something he could use to provide for his future family. He was told that he needed to grow up, and set aside his art as a hobby, and chose something else as his future career.*

Yet Art has always been his passion. It is what inspires him and helps him to process life. Thankfully, he didn't just set it aside. This has blessed many people and has provided for our family for years in ways we never would have expected.

We don't get to choose our children's passions. It is for us to support them as they seek to develop and use them.

If our children don't appear to have any passion for anything. Give it time. Be interesting, Invite interesting people into your life. Expose your children to interesting things. Most of all be patient and not pushy. Interests and passion will come in their due time.

WHERE CAN I FIND AFFORDABLE TRAINING COURSES FOR MY CHILDREN TO LEARN SPECIFIC SKILLS

The answer to this really depends on what sort of training your child is looking for. If it is computer based, such as Graphic Design, Programing, Animations, Photo Editing, Excel, etc., then there are so many great online courses available.

While some of these online courses cost money, you can often find them on sale. Others are completely free or low cost. Also in cases like Lynda.com you may be able to access these for free via your local library. So check and see if that is an option before paying full price.

As far as other types of technical training, look in your community. There may be local classes available. If you know someone in the field your child is interested in, talk to the person and ask for advice in how to prepare and where they can go to learn those skills.

HOW CAN I FIND INTERNSHIP/APPRENTICESHIP OPPORTUNITIES

Many internships and apprenticeship opportunities come from person contact. Find your teen's interest.

When entering into an apprenticeship or internship agreement, commit to writing the expectations and parameters of the apprenticeship or internship. This prevents misunderstandings. Whether this is free for experience or paid, this is not for the purpose of just having an unpaid or low pay employee.

This is a learning experience. Traditionally, apprentices learn the job from the ground up, doing the menial, but important work of maintenance. They learn every facet they can. So, when they leave, they understand the various needed aspects of running the trade or business.

Have your teen check local businesses to see if they can do an internship or apprenticeship there. Have your teen ask small business owners, if your teen can work in an internship or apprenticeship, for them.

Check with friends. Ask if they know someone who does what your teen is interested in.

Donna- *I had a friend who was an author. Julia and I took a fiction writing class from here. Julia showed interest and was invited to be an apprentice and learn how to be a research assistant to her. Julia gained valuable experience researching and compiling the research.*

Another friend apprenticed to a local stained glass artist, as a teen. He gained extensive knowledge of the field and developed great skill. As an adult, he developed his own studio and his own stained glass business.

Currently, my grandson has apprenticed in his father's rocket company. He is learning what engineers do and learning about the space industry.

Some internships pay, others do not, but they give a youth opportunity to gain experience.

HOW CAN I HELP MY CHILD CREATE AN IMPRESSIVE PORTFOLIO

Homeschool Portfolios can come in many shapes and sizes. Here are the most common portfolios you can help your high schooler prepare and create.

CURRICULUM VITAE

This is a "brief" one-page overview of their qualifications, education, GPA, training, experience, extra-curricular activities, awards, community involvement, and test scores.

TRANSCRIPT

This is a list of areas studied arranged as subject, grade, and credits. This would include any courses taken from accredited institutions and any college courses completed. Third level courses and college courses are honors level.

CLASSIC PORTFOLIO

This can be plain or annotated and is more in depth than either a curriculum Vitae or Transcript. Portfolios can include lists of literature read, museums visited, cultural arts experienced, experiments conducted, as well as details of apprenticeships, campaigns, and other community involvement. They can also include a summary of courses taken that are not accredited, as they can show skill sets obtained.

An annotated portfolio might include one page essays on books read and other essays associated with lists in the portfolio, as well as study goals, and a learning record. A curriculum vitae, transcript, and simple portfolio can be impressive, especially when "Detailed Annotated Portfolio is Available on Request," is at the bottom of the simple portfolio.

Art students build a portfolio of representative works, knowing that they will be judged by the worst piece that they include in their portfolio. Why? Because their worst piece represents the worst they are likely to do. Music and theater students often include a selection of their performance.

Many of the programs in the arts are selective and competitive by portfolio, after they meet the university standard for entry.

10. HOW DO I HOMESCHOOL WITHOUT HAVING IT TAKE OVER MY LIFE?

This is a common concern for many prospective homeschool moms. These moms remember the huge task of caring for their children as babies and toddlers. And in many cases, rejoiced when it was time to send their children to school. Why? They felt that they had paid their motherhood dues, and could finally have "Me" time to rediscover who they are, without having their children attached to their hip, every waking moment.

Now that they are looking into homeschooling, a common fear for many mothers is that they will once again, lose themselves in the needs of their children. They fear that they will be required to oversee every moment of their children's homeschool day, as they imagine is the case with their children's public school teachers.

There are four important things we want to discuss pertaining to this topic.

1. Your children's teachers aren't sitting right next to your child all day long, overseeing every aspect of their school day. There are times they are teaching, times they are helping, and times your children and the other students in the class are given an assignment by their teacher, such as reading and writing, and set to do their work independently at their desk, while the teacher sits at her desk, working on her own work, such as, grading papers.

2. While babies and toddlers naturally require a lot of time, attention and monitoring your school aged children do not. Oh, they all need time and attention, but nothing like when they were solely dependent on you.

3. Homeschooling doesn't take all day. As we discussed earlier in this book, for younger children homeschool days should only be 2-4 hours tops. For older children the time increases, but so does the amount of time spent in independent studies.

This is why it is vital that mothers schedule in, non-negotiable, mom care time every day. We have a whole chapter about mom care in our last book, *A Beginner's Guide for Homeschooling*, where we discuss mom care because it is so important for the functioning of your homeschool.

HOW DO I HOMESCHOOL AND KEEP A HOME, TOO?

You should not be doing all the work, while your children entertain themselves, or are occupied by a screen. When toddlers see you working and want to help, let them. They will learn a lot and get faster and more efficient in their help.

TAKE TIME TO TRAIN YOUR CHILDREN TO DO FIVE THINGS:

1. Make their bed upon, as soon as possible upon waking up. If they live in a humid climate they can turn down their covers to air the bed while getting breakfast. If they live in a dry climate they can make it right away.

2. Properly put clean laundry neatly away, in its proper place, as soon as it is received. It does not go on the floor, stacked on the dresser, or bed.

3. Place dirty laundry in the hamper immediately after taking the dirty clothes off.

4. Place trash in the trash can, do not leave it for someone else to pick up. Don't be a litterbug!

5. Promptly and properly put projects, books, and toys away, before pulling out more stuff, going on to other activities or leaving to play.

When children are trained to do these five things and gain

these habits, your children will know how to bring order into their life, the home will be less of a stress, and much easier to manage.

Habit training is not telling them or giving them a list. It is being the example and then helping do the pattern regularly until it is automatic. A routine is a string of simple habits, done in sequence.

This takes a little time at first but pays dividends!

Include your children in shared family work. Teach children how to set the table and make basic condiments, such as salad dressing. Let children help in meal preparations. After the meal, have everyone bring their plate, cup, bowl, and utensils to the sink, rinse them, and stack them as they are able. Have everyone help clear the table and learn how to put foods and condiments away in the fridge.

This makes mealtime preparations and cleanup as a family more enjoyable. Mom is not doing it all! No child is left behind, isolated in the kitchen, working alone, while everyone else runs off to do their own thing.

In the evening, before the bedtime routine, work together as a family to do a quick pick up of the house and make sure toys and other things used during the day are stored in their proper place.

This way, mom is not staying up later to pick up and everyone helps. You wake up to a clean kitchen and a tidy house! We have more easy and helpful ideas in book one, *A Beginner's Guide for Homeschooling.*

HOW DO I HOMESCHOOL AND WORK FROM HOME?

While working from home and homeschooling can be a balancing act at times, it is totally doable. We say this from both personal experience, as well as observation.

To be successful with both work and homeschool, a key element is simple basic consistent routines and schedules, that help our day move smoothly.

ROUTINES

Routines are daily habits, strung together in a sequence. For instance, every morning we wake up, get dressed, make our beds, and eat breakfast, etc.

Simple basic routines include personal routines, home & family management, & homeschool

MOM'S PERSONAL ROUTINES

Morning Routine

- Personal Scripture Study & Prayer
- Affirmation
- Vision for the Day
- Exercise

- Scribe - Journal and Morning Pages
- Shower
- Groom & Dress
- Make bed
- Brush teeth after breakfast

Evening Routine

- Turn off screens 1-2 hours before bedtime
- Walk or do four minute exercise routine
- Write in business journal
- Brush Teeth
- Pray
- Read
- Sleep

CHILDREN'S PERSONAL ROUTINES

Morning Routine

- Get Dressed
- Make Bed
- Eat Breakfast
- Brush Teeth
- Read

Evening Routine

- Bathe (if needed) and cleanup after finished
- Get dressed for Bed
- Brush Teeth
- Use Bathroom
- Pray

- Have Family Read Aloud Time
- Sleep

HOME & FAMILY MANAGEMENT

Below are two examples of Home & Family management routines as done in both Donna's and Julia's homes.

Donna's Home & Family Management Routines:

Morning routine

- *Get laundry in motion- once in motion, keep in motion. Use the timer to let you know when a load finishes. When the dryer stops, stop what you are doing and take the ten- minute break to fold, hang up, and completely put the load away. Do it together as a family. We start a load of laundry before bed. Then transfer it to the dryer and start another load in the morning. By the time breakfast and meal prep is done, loads are ready to be addressed.*

- *Prep and Clean Up after Breakfast*

- *Early Lunch & Dinner Preparation- What can be collected to the kitchen and what can be prepared early.*

Midday Routine

- *Make lunch together*
- *Clean up lunch together*
- *Quiet time*

Evening Routine - Family Time

- *Tidy the house together*
- *Evening Read Aloud*
- *Family Prayer*

Julia's Home & Family Management Routines:

Our home management routines often happen during morning routine times, meal prep times and bedtimes, and overseen by mom and dad, including children in the work.

- *While the children are getting ready for the day I start laundry that we just process as needed throughout the day*

- *Meals are made together with children as helpers.*

- *Dishes are done as a family after each meal.*

- *Home clean up is as needed. A final clean up during evening routine times so we can go to bed in a clean home.*

HOMESCHOOL ROUTINES

Below are two examples of Homeschooling Routines as done in both Donna's and Julia's homes.

Donna Homeschool Routines:

Daily   *Walk*
First Hour - *Power of an Hour Block*
- *Scripture*
- *Classic Read Aloud*
- *Gateway to learning –*
  Sunday- Person of Faith & Character Theme of the Week

Monday - Artist of the Month, Artwork of the Week, Art Term of the Week, and Spelling Rule of the Week

Tuesday- Musician of the Month, Musical Piece of the Week, Musical Term of the Week, and Grammar Rule of the Week

Wednesday- Mathematician & Math Concept of the Week or Scientist & Science Concept of the Week

Thursday- World Leader of the Week, Language Arts - Roots & Affix of the Week, and Nation of the Week

Friday - Poet of the Month, Poem of the Week, Poetry Term of the Week, State of the Week, and Geography Term of the week.

Second Hour-*Skill Development Block*

- *One-on-one Mentoring and Tutoring, at their need and pace.*

- *Independent Learning -using skills and honing skills through self-selected, interest-led learning projects and activities*

- *Recess - self-directed imaginative and physical play to help develop executive function.*

As my children grew, they needed me less for tutorial and more for mentoring. We still continued scripture study and read aloud. Older children took more time in afternoons to personal study.

Julia's Homeschool Routines:

Family Work Out

Family Meditation

Reading
- *Our eldest two split their time between reading scripture &*

chapter books.

- *Our youngest splits his time between reading lessons, reading his beginner books & getting read to.*

Writing/Typing
- *Every other day we work on writing and every other day on typing skills.*

Math
- *We break out into one on one with our children for math. My husband will work with our oldest son & I work with our daughter.*

- *The youngest plays quietly in the same room while we work, usually, building block castles.*

Geography/Interest Based Studies
- *Every other day we do a Geography Lesson. Our children work on researching and filling out their US Geography printables we created.*

- *Every other day our children work on doing interest based studies. Last year our daughter worked on creative writing and our son on programming.*

- *Again our youngest often plays quietly during this time with building blocks, coloring, imaginative play with stuffed animals.*

Documentaries
- *We end our day with a documentary most days, rotating between Science, Geography, Animals, and History.*
- *While our children watch their documentary we work nearby.*
- *After they are done with the documentary they come and report 3-4 things they learned and we have a long discussion.*

LUNCH (school is out)

Some days we will do a hands-on project or experiment in place of the documentary. Library trips, and museums trips are once a week on

Friday. *Which is our school out day. Our children do slightly longer days M-TH to have Friday off.*

SCHEDULES

Schedules are a very important aspect for balancing homeschool and work from home. Schedules determine when we school, work and play.

Below are two different examples of our Homeschool/Work schedules to meet our different needs and family dynamics.

Julia's Schedule:

We have found in our family, that having a basic schedule for when we wake up, wake our children up, have meals, start school, end school, and go to bed, helps a lot with the smooth running of our home, school and work.

We have a set wake up time for our children to start their day and a schedule for lights out Bedtime.

My husband is a morning person and I am more of a night person. So, my husband likes to get up early in the morning to get in uninterrupted work time before the family wakes up. I like to stay up after the family is in bed, to get in my uninterrupted work time.

For our work during the day we get in several hours, while tag teaming who stops to take care of our children's needs. We are able to work during school hours, sitting near our children while they are engaged in independent studies.

Then after school we are able to get more work done in our office, while our children play until dinner. After dinner is family time.

Here is our basic schedule

5:30- 7 AM Dad Work Time
7 -8 AM Wake up & do morning routine
8- 12 Homeschool
12 Lunch
After Lunch - Dinner Prep (and home clean up) Time Children Play while Husband & I Work
5:30 Dinner
After dinner - FamilyTime (we play games, go on family walks, play outside, and watch movies)
8 PM Bedtime Routine
9 PM Lights Out
9-10 PM Mom & Dad time
10-11:30 Mom work time

Donna's Schedule:

When I homeschooled my children and when I homeschool grandchildren while their parents travel this was my basic schedule. This was my schedule after my last child was sleeping through the night!

Before that, I was not working from home and due to colic in my baby keeping the household up to 4:00 am. So, we slept in and did homeschool after lunch, at that time.

Here is our basic schedule

4:45 - 8:00   Rise, my morning routine, and work for mom.
8:00 - 9:00   Breakfast & current events, get laundry in motion, and meal prep
9:00 -10:00   Family walk
10:00 - Noon   Homeschool
Noon - 1:00   Lunch and Clean up

1:00 to 2:30	*Quiet time for children, work for mom*
2:30 to 5:30	*Free time for children, work for mom*
5:30 to 6:00	*Dinner*
6:00 to 9:00	*Family time and evening routines.*
9:00	*Lights out*

In the end, it is for you to decide what routines and schedules you will put into place for homeschool, work and family times.

The important thing is to make your schedule and routines a habit, which will help everything run smoother and allow you to fulfill all your responsibilities.

HOW DO I HOMESCHOOL WITHOUT BECOMING INVISIBLE?

Many moms, as caregivers, may feel invisible. Too often, it is our own fault. Here are some ways to prevent this from happening.

NINE WAYS TO NOT BE INVISIBLE

1. Schedule self-care. So many moms take care of themselves, only if they have time and energy left after taking care of home and family. Moms, you do not find time, you make time! You should not be invisible to you.

2. Train your children in how to work, so they are helpful and you are not doing everything.
You are not the family maid. Work with your children, they are not your maid either.

3. Train your family in being respectful. Speak to them in the same way you want them to speak and treat you. If you forget, acknowledge, apologize, and try again. When they forget, say with a smile, "Nice try. Let's try that again with more kindness and respect."

4. Establish basic routines that become your default. A default happens, unless disrupted by something else more important, then after the interruption, the routine returns to its rightful place. For instance, after sickness or visitors leave, the routine resumes.

5. Train your Husband. It is OK to communicate your needs to your husband! Let him know what your love language is. And let him know that it is important to be acknowledged for your hard work.

6. Don't be a yes mom! It is OK to say NO! You can be gracious, of course. "Thank you for thinking of me, I will have to decline at this time." Do not let yourself get overscheduled. Even doing one thing for each child can be overwhelming at times. So, be wise with your time. As you are, you will discover the abundance of "less is more."

7. Pursue developing your own talents and interests, even if it is only a few minutes here and a few minutes there. Set goals in developing those talents. You won't be invisible as you shine!

8. Connect with other adults. But do not get sucked into scrolling social media for interaction. Have some moms join you for lunch, Girls night outs, Book clubs, support groups, etc.

9. Take time to serve others. Invite your children to help. When we are outside ourselves, lifting others, we are letting our light shine.

HOW CAN I HANDLE MY CHILDREN THAT MANY HOURS?

As we have stated earlier in this book, homeschooling should only take between 2-4 hours a day tops, for younger children. As your children get older, the length in time increases, but at that point more of their time is taken up in independent study. Which doesn't require your constant oversight.

Handling your children for just a couple hours a day for homeschool is doable. Especially when your homeschool day is broken into time blocks. You can take breaks between as needed, which makes a huge difference.

After homeschool time, encourage your children to play, develop interests and be kids. If your children are being particularly trying, and are driving you crazy, consider sending them outside to play for a bit, it's good for them. If you don't have a fenced yard to do this, consider taking them on a walk or to a park. Trust me it helps.

Yes, it is an adjustment to having your children once again home with you all day. However, soon you will fall into your daily routines and find that you actually love having your children home with you.

HOW DO I HOMESCHOOL WHILE TRAVELING?

We both have done a lot of traveling with our families while homeschooling our children. Homeschooling actually makes it so much easier to travel as a family. You don't have to worry about the hassle of checking your children out of school, missing important classes, tests or assignments.

Donna - *I wanted my children to meet extended family, see the family history sites, American History sites, and natural wonders, before they left our home and went into the world.*

So, when my two oldest graduated the same day from high school, I proposed a big adventure. My husband felt we could not afford it. I wanted to make it happen, so I proposed camping at state parks and that I would prepare the food. I got AAA guide-books for each state. They had points of interest and historical information.

We left on Memorial Day and returned in July, six weeks later. We traversed a continent and traveled over 12,000 miles. We only stayed in a hotel two nights. Otherwise, we camped, visited relatives, or friends. We saw natural wonders, experienced museums, learned history, and experienced America.

This was a grand trip on a shoestring! The AAA Guidebooks informed us of free museums, free sites to see, and places to camp. We kept a trip journal. But for the most part, the trip, venues, and socialization they gained that was their curriculum.

When we were in Washington DC my fifteen year-old son saw a girl with a T-Shirt that read, "Only after the last flower is paved over..." He told me, "Only someone who had never left the city would believe such."

They got to really be socialized by family, friends and relatives along the way. They also got the socialization of meeting people at the different venues across the country, both those running the venues and visiting them.

They learned History, Geography, and even Science. We had wonderful memories of Mom & Dad's Great Adventure to cherish. That was the first of many major adventures, often during the school year, during off season.

Julia - *One of the reasons we chose to homeschool was, so we could travel more. At which point the world became our school in an amazing way.*

We have traveled all over the United States with our children, and at one point, lived in various countries in Europe for six months, just because we could. Throughout our journeys, it has been easy to bring our laptops, a few books and materials to do our school work with us, wherever we went.

Additionally, as we would visit new places, we would always take the time to learn about their history, their culture, and anything of interest about the people and places. We would go to museums, and historical sites and try to immerse ourselves, if only briefly, in the places we went.

Traveling has actually made homeschooling easier. How? Well, as we have traveled we have found that our children have been inspired to learn about many things they otherwise wouldn't know about.

When traveling during a school year, we recommend bringing with you, your official homeschool documents, in the case you ever need to prove you are authorized to homeschool.

Also, be aware of the homeschooling laws for where you are visiting. We had no problem while in Europe, as most people figured we were tourists on holiday.

However, there are certain states in the US that have it in their laws that if you are residing in their states border for x amount of time, often over a month, then you are subject to their homeschool laws, even if your children are registered as homeschoolers, in your home state.

IN CLOSING

It is our deepest hope, that you have found the answers you were looking for, within pages of this book. We know that making the choice to homeschool can be scary, especially when you have questions that you can't find answers to.

Homeschooling, like with any educational forum is a work in progress. Because there is no such thing as a one size fits all, it will take you time to figure out what works best for you and your family.

Be patient. Breathe. Let go of your anxiety. Know that you are not alone in this. Take the time to explore and discover. If you do this, you will find that homeschooling your children can be the best thing you could do for your family.

If you still have questions and concerns about homeschooling, we invite you to read the other books in this series.

ABOUT THE AUTHORS

JULIA ANN GROVES

Julia Groves is the third of seven children born to Roger and Donna Goff. She was born in Colorado, but raised predominantly in Utah. Julia was homeschooled from 6th grade through highschool after which she attended George Wythe College. Though she did not formally graduate with a degree, she did maintain a 3.98 GPA during her studies at George Wythe and values what she learned while attending there.

Julia married her best friend Rory Groves in March of 2009 and together they have three young children. In addition to homeschooling their children, Julia and her husband also run their own business. (Rory is an illustrator and Julia runs a family lifestyle site where she enjoys creating resources for today's mom.) In 2015, Julia and Rory sold their home and most of their possessions to travel full time with their children. They spent 6 months living abroad in Europe and then returned back to the US. Though their travels have now slowed down and they are once again looking to settle down in a home that love of travel is still there.

As a born storyteller, Julia has always been fascinated with history, art, different cultures and meeting new people. Additionally, Julia enjoys photography, cooking, experiencing new things, teaching, reading, crafting, travel and graphic design.

DONNA GOFF

Donna Goff and her husband, Roger, are parents of seven children and have homeschooled since the 1980s. They are the grandparents to thirteen grandchildren, twelve living. Donna earned her BA in Fine Art & Design; Drawing & Painting; and earned her MA Ed in 2008 while homeschooling her youngest three children.

She has worked to give homeschool support since 1983 and has been active in presenting at homeschool conferences around the US since 1995.

Donna loves to spend time with her family, to enjoy nature with her family, and spending time with friends. In her spare time, she loves to create art, cook, sew, garden, DIY, sing, write, is an avid walker and enjoys learning new things.

www.ingramcontent.com/pod-product-compliance
Lightning Source LLC
Chambersburg PA
CBHW061726020426
42331CB00006B/1108